SELL LIKE A WOMAN

*Harness Your Feminine
Superpowers So That You Can
Sell With Ease… Not Sleaze*

Suzi Seddon

Sell Like A Woman

© 2024 Suzi Seddon

All rights reserved. No part of this book may be reproduced, stored in a retrieval system or transmitted in any form or by any means (electronic, mechanical, photocopy, recording, scanning or other) except for brief quotations in critical reviews or articles, without the prior written permission of the publisher.

ISBN: 9781738480005 Paperback

Published by: Inspired By Publishing

Cover Designed By: Tanya Grant, The TNG Designs Group Limited

The strategies in this book are presented primarily for enjoyment and educational purposes. Every effort has been made to trace copyright holders and obtain their permission for the use of copyright material.

The information and resources provided in this book are based upon the authors' personal experiences. Any outcome, income statements or other results, are based on the authors' experiences and there is no guarantee that your experience will be the same. There is an inherent risk in any business enterprise or activity and there is no guarantee that you will have similar results as the author as a result of reading this book.

The author reserves the right to make changes and assumes no responsibility or liability whatsoever on behalf of any purchaser or reader of these materials.

ACKNOWLEDGEMENTS

Nikola Tesla – the physics genius and inventor extraordinaire. What an inspiration he is for all who appreciate that energy is everything.

Bruce Lee – who many consider the most influential martial artist of all time. In his short time on earth he created over 330 quotes before he died aged just 32. A go to source for mental clarity when you feel you need it.

Nadja Swarovski – great, great, granddaughter of the founder of Swarovski Crystal and was the first female member of the executive board, responsible for spreading the appeal of the product into the exciting plethora of spangled items it can be used for today. A true visionary, trailblazer and innovator in her field.

My Mum, at 99 years old, 'the' biggest influence in my life.

Table of Contents

INTRODUCTION 1
    THE MAGIC 8
    THE METHOD 11

PART 1 13

THE MAGIC 13

CHAPTER 1 15
    HOW MEN SELL AND WHY IT WORKS FOR THEM 15
    HOW SELLING LIKE A MAN CAN KILL YOUR
    BUSINESS 18

CHAPTER 2 23
    FINDING YOUR ZONE OF GENIUS 23
    WHAT WILL PEOPLE PAY FOR IN BUSINESS? 28
    MAKING THE CHOICE 30

CHAPTER 3 33
    VALUES 33
    BELIEFS 37
    IMPOSTER SYNDROME 41
    NEGATIVITY 43
    PROGRESSIVE THINKING 47

CHAPTER 4 51
    LETTING GO 51
    SOUL SISTERS 54
    BUILD RELATIONSHIPS 57

CHAPTER 5 61
    GRABBING ATTENTION 61
    THE POWER OF STORY 65

CHAPTER 6 71
    MAGNETICALLY ATTRACT EXACTLY WHO YOU
    WANT TO WORK WITH 71
    AUDIENCE MAKEUP 74

CHAPTER 7 77
    BRINGING THE PIECES TOGETHER 77

CHAPTER 8 85
   GLADIATOR HORMONES TO THE RESCUE 85
   BREATHE EASY 87

CHAPTER 9 91
   GETTING UNSTUCK & MOVING FORWARD 91
   VISUALISE SUCCESS AND PLAN FOR IT 93

CHAPTER 10 97
   AVOIDING BURNOUT & OVERWHELM 97
   PLANNING TO MANAGE OVERWHELM 100

CHAPTER 11 105
   FREQUENCIES 105
   GIVING OFF GOOD VIBRATIONS 108
   ENTHUSIASM IS INFECTIOUS 112

PART 2 .... ERROR! BOOKMARK NOT DEFINED.

THE METHOD .... ERROR! BOOKMARK NOT DEFINED.

CHAPTER 12 119
   OPENING THE FLOW STATE 119

CHAPTER 13 125
   THE POWERBASE 125

CHAPTER 14 129
   SCRAP THE SCRIPT – ESPECIALLY WHEN COLD
   CALLING 129

CHAPTER 15 135
   UNCOVERING THE CORE ISSUES 135
   SLOW DOWN TO SPEED UP 140
   MAP YOUR OFFER TO THEIR ISSUES 141

CHAPTER 16 145
   THE PITCH 145
   PRESENTING OPTIONS 146
   DIAGNOSIS AND THE WAY FORWARD 149

CHAPTER 17 153
   PACKAGING YOUR VALUE 153

CHAPTER 18 .... **159**
   BUILDING TRUST... 159
   BODY LANGUAGE.. 161

CHAPTER 19 .... **165**
   EMBRACE REJECTION & BUILD RESILIENCE............. 165

CHAPTER 20 .... **169**
   OVERCOMING OBJECTIONS 169

CHAPTER 21 .... **175**
   SELL, TRACK, CELEBRATE & REPEAT 175

CHAPTER 22 .... **179**
   TRIP WIRES! 179

CONCLUSION **187**

INVITATION.. **193**

INTRODUCTION

How would you like to 10X your leads today?

This is the top question that many seek the answer to when entering the world of sales. Without leads, there is no life blood to future proof your business. Without new leads, are you purely relying on recommendations and word of mouth referrals to grow your business?

As important as this question is, there is more important work to do first so that you avoid chasing rainbows by not doing the preliminary work required for your business to be built on rock and not on sand.

When I began to write this book, I literally went into a stream of consciousness and asked myself "what do you need to know about selling?". The result is the book you see before you. An amalgamation of over 30 years of my sales experience and observations in selling.

So, why Sell Like a Woman?

Feminine energy is incredibly powerful but over many years our guiding light has been hidden, principally because most sales training has traditionally been taught using masculine energy rather than our core feminine energy. Women have struggled between coming from their centre and trying to adapt to using more masculine strategies and techniques because they don't feel authentic to us.

This was my experience too. It just didn't sit right with me. It was way too prescriptive and there was a very obvious mismatch that meant I couldn't get into my flow at all. I was being driven by a process that didn't fit with my natural style. My magic was extinguished.

Luckily as a shy 16 year old I had had the great good fortune to get a job as a Saturday girl for an amazing lady called Kay who was a university lecturer, whose own dream was to run a craft shop filled with fluffy animals, hand-thrown pottery, handmade wooden toys, and even Paddington Bears! I honestly thought it was going to be an easy gig just standing behind the counter and occasionally ringing up a sale or two. Within the first hour it became obvious things were going to work very differently and very soon I learnt my first lesson; being coaxed out from behind the counter, encouraged to engage with customers. Surprisingly I quickly started to really enjoy my work. Kay insisted I knew the backstory to all the artists and crafters who supplied their wares to the shop so that I could answer questions with confidence and make suggestions too. Soon I learnt I could take them from casual browsers to happy buyers. What I couldn't have known at that age was how valuable that on-the-job training was and how that influenced my future more than I could ever have imagined.

This opened my eyes to understanding my own personal magic and over time, I became adept at weaving it into the lives of the people I touched to not only serve them in the best way I could but also influence their choices for the better too.

I also realised how valuable my new skill was and soon I couldn't wait to get stuck in to a proper role in sales to pay the rent for my first flat. So I took an evening job, selling timeshare appointments! Now this is a really tough ask; ringing people who were not expecting my call and getting them to attend a 3-hour sales appointment, hours away from where they lived, for something that at the beginning of the call they had never heard of! But you know what, I LOVED IT. I learnt so much about cold calling... and rejection too. I learnt about confidence, resilience, enthusiasm, humour in sales and the power of just being me. I was enough!

By the 1990's I had begun work as a secretary in an office that demanded all women wore skirts to work! We were still subjected to the rules set by our exclusively male bosses at that time. Needless to say, there was little opportunity yet to be a female boss but slowly we started to make our own demands (not least, trousers in the office!).

In those early years I struggled with my confidence levels, especially in front of people who exuded bucket loads with such ease. So I moved to work as a personal assistant for a company selling office equipment solutions. I handled all the administration including inviting people my boss wanted to interview for sales roles. Many of them embodied ludicrous levels of smarminess.... AND they got the job! What was all that about??! Confidence, it would appear, counted for a lot.

By now I was married and my income made a real impact on our household finances, it gave our household 'choices'. Money does, in fact, give you choices. With a bit more security behind me, I made my move into 'sales proper' and joined a recruitment company where I really blossomed into the role of sales at warp speed and I never looked back.

Realising I was enough and that I really could do well in sales was a pivotal moment for me. As you can hear, I had also been through a lot of soul searching, confidence building and imposter syndrome busting. But it was only then that I realised I sold in a totally different way to my male colleagues. Over the years that followed, I gathered together the fragments of the jigsaw forming in front of me, until I had ultimate clarity of what the nuances were in the way I uniquely sold.

This lies at the heart of Sell Like a Woman. It's about being or getting in touch with yourself, understanding how to manage your own energy and the vital lessons to becoming mega successful in selling. You'll really dig into finding where you own magic lies and understand the difference between competence and expertise to find your market niche or even micro-niche to sell to. You will discover what drives you in terms of beliefs and values and how this relates to your business and everyone who works in it. You will become clear on your marketing message so you are always clear and concise in your communications and of course we will delve into mindset, which is a massive piece of being successful in sales. That's why I dedicate the first 11 chapters to unpacking lessons that could literally move mountains for you in terms of self-worth and confidence.

So, I have split the content between THE MAGIC and THE METHOD.

The Magic will help you distil where your own brand of magic and superpowers lie, whilst working in tandem on your mindset.

The Method is my simple framework to follow, putting you and your business front and centre without you feeling you are being pushy or manipulative.

So many women I've mentored struggled with sales. Both the mindset and the strategy. They had tried to emulate the loud and pushy sales tactics born in the 80s that still survives today, and it left them feeling icky and preferring to avoid selling altogether. Instead, I teach a way of selling that feels natural and invites our customers in – rather than manhandling them to the checkout.

The Magic and The Method are intertwined. You need both to excel.

If you struggle with the whole concept of selling, then this book is for you. Perhaps you are a quiet achiever; an expert in your field who wants a comfortable way to attract your ideal prospects. In my 12 month immersion programme I take you through the whole process, step by step and at the end you will have a personalised sales process that you can adapt to your business but at the same time authentically reflects you as a professional woman in business. No persuasion or icky, pushy sales tactics here. You'll simply become a master influencer who serves their audience hard but sells EASY.

> *"You can't hide behind a counter, a webinar, sales page or a website and wait for the sales to come to you.*
>
> *You can't sit back and wait for opportunities to appear!*
>
> *You need to speak from your centre with clarity, confidence and certainty - that is where the magic meets the mettle."*
>
> *- Suzi Seddon*

THE MAGIC

More women than ever have stepped into running a business today than in the last 30+ years. Right now, the world needs our creativity in business because simply put, there is a gaping hole just waiting for us to fill it. As individuals, women explore our vision from a more intuitive, collaborative source. We build a connection with people naturally and it matters because it makes it personal. No manipulation, no pushiness... just a feminine energy strategy to make lots of sales without the ick.

In years past, we had to fit into a man's world (anyone remember power suits and massive shoulder pads?). During the war years our place had been largely at home, nurturing our children and building a home life for our men to return to. After the war, this male hierarchy system transferred almost intact into the workplace. Women, however, were not factored in to be a part of it.

We struggled to find our place in the world of business where we could slot in. This often meant in a secretarial capacity. This was where I started out. It wasn't a very welcoming place and we were often met with hostility and regarded as taking jobs from the men.

The fact was that we were so busy trying to fit in that we didn't stand out in our own right.

Many succumbed to creating an alternative identity for themselves; a more masculine look and with it the 'alpha female' was born. For many it seemed the only way to be if you wanted to be taken seriously in business. Offices across the world were a swathe of black power suits and crisp white shirts, not a peep of pink or femininity in sight.

As a new century loomed, we began to tap into the whispers inside of us, to have the courage to step out of convention and into our own power as women in business.

Today it is our soft skills that are needed. No one wants to be hard sold to, to be manipulated or pushed into a decision to buy. This is the gap we can step into with ease. We already possess both the business nous and the soft skills to succeed. This is the void that exists in many male dominated sales operations that leave people feeling, quite frankly, unheard and unloved.

We are living through extraordinary times and challenges that many are unprepared for, especially in the world of business and entrepreneurship. As buyers of products and services we want to know more about the person we are dealing with. We <u>want</u> to trust, but before we can do that, we <u>need</u> to feel heard and that takes us to the very heart of where we need to start our discussion here.

The Magic teaches about the background of selling and sales so that the reader can avoid some of the pitfalls of selling and experience more of the highs. This is not an exhaustive list but it does highlight the areas I have found most effective. The sands of time have shifted and today we do things in a totally different way to 30+ years ago. However, it is useful to know the background, not least because your prospects may have grown up in that time zone too.

As you are reading the first part, you may find yourself wondering "how does this relate to selling like a woman?" All of it does, because you have to find the magic within you before you can sell it.

THE METHOD

The Method unwraps my selling system; The Flow State Selling System. I concentrate on teaching you how to sell in flow, how to listen acutely and really get used to using your intuition and inner wisdom. How to ask really good questions to uncover golden nuggets of information. How to navigate objections elegantly and of course, how to secure the sale. The Method is about the process. It's a simple but very effective structure that still allows you to be YOU so that you sell from your centre.

It is an interesting fact that most sales coaches and trainers are men. Their prime energy is masculine and this is the only way most of them know how to sell, by utilising a strong focussed masculine energy.

Women fundamentally sell differently. We have different languaging and an entirely different approach. We know this from years of being on the other side of masculine energy selling to us. So, this is the gap I am stepping into, to teach you how to gain confidence, to feel you have arrived at a place you belong without any trace of imposter syndrome, where you can demonstrate your feminine superpowers for the first time to really Sell Like a Woman.

READY TO UNLOCK YOUR OWN MAGIC?

PART 1

THE MAGIC

SHINE YOUR OWN TORCH

CHAPTER 1
HOW MEN SELL AND WHY IT WORKS FOR THEM

There is a clear difference between how men typically sell and how women sell and this shows up in how we like to buy too.

Men often love to fix things and many love clear instructions and an A-Z process to follow.

Women, generally speaking, hate instructions and some of us find the process stifling. We ride on the wave of our emotions and tune into our intuition and somehow that just doesn't quite fit with following a hard and fast process. But we do love a framework. It allows us more flex to weave our magic whilst keeping on track.

I started my formal career in sales in 1990 and in my first few years selling I was definitely in the serious minority as a woman in sales. I was very much a woman in a man's world. I remember being given a presenter pack which was made up of multiple printed A4 bullet-pointed sheets that could be assembled into a triangular on-the-go desk presentation tool. That fed right into the world of masculine selling (one step down from the trusty clipboard) and far away from the flexible framework that feminine energy flourishes within. Sales men generally love to follow a detailed structure and this was a natural invention by the upper echelons of management to help support them.

Needless to say, I wasn't a supporter of the presenter pack. I found it unwieldy – actually it was a bit like fighting with a Rubik's Cube to put it together in under 10 seconds. Importantly I also observed my own delivery of the information I was sharing was rather stayed – a bit like reading a script. I felt restricted. It also made my prospect totally focus on the Presenter Pack and not engage with me at all! Worst of all, my sales collapsed, and it took me weeks to piece things together with what was happening and snap back into my core feminine energy.

People love to chat and in sales, we need to give them the opportunity to do that. They REALLY love to 'chew the fat' as my Dad would say. He was one man who understood the feminine energy system to really get to know his prospects and keep his customers buying, male or female. He understood the importance of communication and I don't mean the buttoned up, factual delivery approach. I mean how to really chew the fat, chatting leisurely, reminiscing, and debating in equal measure. My Dad was a Master of this and luckily, I learned from the best, practically by osmosis.

Sadly, I would say that men that tune into the masculine energy are still much less inclined to get involved in the emotion of the sale and this is where the gap opens up for women to step into with our natural superpowers, the ones we were born with; warmth, conversation, open questions, nurturing, intuition, listening, being interested, creative thinking and problem solving.

It is important for women to understand how we differ from a man when selling and why, because it opens up a new understanding. This stops us trying to fit in and instead work out where the gaps are and look at how we can stand out. We can then find our own place and pace that empowers us to lead from the front and win business elegantly.

Speaking from your centre with clarity, confidence and certainty is where the magic meets the mettle.

Our biggest secret weapon of influence is our feminine energy which we have learnt to layer on top of the masculine energy we grew up being surrounded by.

HOW SELLING LIKE A MAN CAN KILL YOUR BUSINESS

In order to understand how to sell, we first need to look into how people buy and the approach that men take and how women differ.

If you possess feminine energy as your core energy then you'll know how, when buying something, we love to explain. To discuss the background as to why we are looking for a particular product or service to buy. Feminine energy doesn't want to be rushed and arm wrestled to the nearest cash register. We want to explore our options and decide for ourselves. We may not even make a decision immediately and decide to revisit on another day. We need certainty before we buy, so when we are the one selling, we strive to ensure we give all the details, all the information.

This is diametrically opposed to how masculine energy buys. It tends toward being a mission rather than a browsing experience. Masculine energy wants to go into the shop, identify that the item they want is there, that it is fit for purpose, then to buy it and leave as soon as possible so that they can do something else more interesting. They operate shopping from much more of a tick list. Logic over emotion.

When it comes to bricks and mortar stores, men talk about going 'to buy' something, women talk about going 'to shop'. The difference is subtle but enormous. Women enjoy assistance when shopping and, if you're anything like me, value the opinion of sales assistants and their product knowledge but will likely walk away if we don't receive help. When someone spends time with us, we feel valued. Women expect to be noticed quickly by a sales assistant and hate it when they get ignored in favour of a conversation with an associate taking precedence. It makes us feel like intruders.

Men also like assistance but that's more to do with finding an item quickly, so unhelpful staff who can't be bothered to check stock levels quickly and efficiently really irritate men who are buying. Then of course, when it comes to finally making the purchase, this needs to happen at warp speed for men to be happy… and obviously, shortly before they run out of the door where parking is available outside the store or very nearby to load purchases into their vehicle.

If you don't do any public speaking it is always important to consider how you come across to prospects. I used to own a jewellery business and my focus was on display of my pieces both at my stand and on myself. I became the walking mannequin and I sold so much jewellery literally from around my neck.

Women like to see how something looks in situ whereas men tend to buy on brand or price.

Both consider price when making a decision but masculine energy tends to choose quality *over* price. I guess I'm talking about known brands being the motivator for the purchase, rather than a white label, lookalike product. Conversely feminine energy likes to hunt out a deal and will seek out the best available offer.

So it is very, very important to sell in the right energy that customers are expecting. To be clear I am not talking to men and to women here, I am talking to the masculine or feminine energy an individual identifies with.

This mismatch becomes very apparent when a woman sells in masculine energy. This approach mixes up masculine and feminine energy. At worst you see the alpha female emerge, often seen by men as a bit of a monster they would rather move away from - a female presenting in a masculine way represents a territorial land grab and will likely be met with caution, lack of engagement or worse still, a shut down.

Basically, it wrong foots a man. Remember men are generally speaking much more visually driven than women, so it throws them off track because the alpha female is masking her core female energy and it just feels off and untrustworthy to them.

Much more appealing to a male prospect, is a woman approaching sales with her feminine energy which is less threatening and importantly, they recognise. Do not mistake this to mean weak or unstructured. There is no need to try and shape shift in an effort to win sales. If you do, you are likely to lose the sale entirely because it feels and in fact IS inauthentic. And there lies the rub… selling like a man and not like a woman destroys trust and can kill business opportunities.

A female presenting in feminine energy ticks all the boxes and more. We listen more and have less need to be heard or hear the sound of our own voices. Too much talking comes under the headings of 'convincing' or 'explaining'. It's your job to know your product inside out and be in a position to answer all questions put to you by prospects.

If you find yourself explaining things, then you need to start swotting up on the details of your product or service because simply put your questions should have been crafted to excavate any concerns your prospect has. This is your responsibility. The decision to buy is theirs.

So how do you do it?

Write a list of 5 questions you can ask in a sales conversation that would replace the need to "explain" or "convince".

Concentrate on asking searching questions that get to the bottom of what the prospect is searching for.

Only in this way can you both understand if your product, programme or service fulfils their need.

CHAPTER 2

People often think that sales is all about scripts, asking for the money and money mindset, but the real magic behind sales is actually selling something that you believe in.

In order to sell like a woman, we first need to look at what you're selling and what opportunities there are available to you.

FINDING YOUR ZONE OF GENIUS

If you are looking to start a business, the opportunity could be a completely new idea or venture or if you're already in business, it could be a different angle to explore a current opportunity that doesn't feel quite dialled in yet.

Our experiences develop our secret sauce and uniqueness so that we can then help others to save time, energy, money and mistakes. Thus, sometimes our zone of genius develops from a place we once had chaos in our own lives.

The clues are there, my friends. We just need to recognise them and pull the golden threads together;

spell casting if you like by bringing our own brand of magic to life.

So, when it comes to new opportunities, you'll probably have a lot of ideas but they all prompt one question:

"Which one do I pick!?"

Maybe you're thinking "I've got several ideas in mind, but which one is best?" Maybe you are thinking "what am I really qualified to talk about?" I used to fall at this post but remember that your experience qualifies you… *not* just a piece of paper!

Maybe you find yourself considering which one will make you the most money?

Even though ensuring the potential audience you have in mind *can* afford your product, programme or service is important, money must not be the paramount driver of your decision. This is a trap many fall into. Today it's very easy to follow the money. Many are focussed on making ends meet. However, the danger is you transform what you do into all work and no play, no fun, with none of your own special sauce that puts a spring in your step each day. Base your decision on passion for your area of expertise or genius. It may sound cliché but you will never work another day in your life because it's what you love and you won't ever see it as work. You will also never run out of ideas because your whole being is geared toward seeking information in relation to it as a matter of course, rather than having to be driven to find more data because you've run dry!

Listen to your heart. When you sell from a place of loving what you do, your natural enthusiasm will shine through. Don't worry about what will make you the most money, that will follow if you love what you do.

As I mentioned earlier, our zone of genius often comes from our own life experiences.

What have you experienced that you could help others with?

Maybe you went on a trek up Everest and could talk authoritatively on the physical and emotional preparation, essential gear needed, medications to take with you, emergency strategies etc.
Perhaps you have been navigating home schooling and could now provide other parents with direction, lesson plans, curriculum stages to adhere to etc.

You will likely have more choices than is initially apparent to you. And you probably have a lot of different experiences.

Our life experiences can provide some of the keys to unlocking the conundrum of your life's purpose. Many of us go through a chunk of our lives having no idea what ours is. Our mess can even be our message if we manage to resolve it! Our experiences give us clues as to what direction we could take, where we can be of service to others and what brings us joy. This can be driven by personal challenge, charity, or just plain old money. But personal joy is a crucial element of success.

Can you imagine writing a pop song that turns into a hit and then having to sing it around the world for the next 30 years if you didn't really like it in the first place!?

Let's not do that. Let's do the work to find the answer for you.

We need to discover which one you feel the most passionate about, the most confident to talk about where words are bursting to get out of your mouth to share.

Activity:

Talk for two minutes about each experience and see how it feels. No preparation, just start talking.

This is when you discover the wealth of knowledge that lies dormant within you. The nuggets of wisdom you have been accumulating and storing away for another day.

So, this exercise requires you to think in stream of consciousness, what you already know off the top of your head. What it is not, is too much analysis on your part when you are answering each question. Don't worry how silly or insignificant your answers are… for example, if flying a kite makes you happy, let's hear it!

When you start to list your life experiences you may start to see similarities in your zone of genius.

To dig deeper into identifying your area of genius, I've created an exercise that you can access in the online resources area. Download "Discover your Zone of Genius" activity at www.suziseddon.com/resources

WHAT WILL PEOPLE PAY FOR IN BUSINESS?

If you're new to business or you're just about to get started, you may find yourself asking the big question:

What will people actually pay me for?

Well the answer is what saves them time... or makes them money.

Saving time can mean following a tried and tested blueprint or a framework to find a more streamlined process or seeking advice from someone who has trodden a similar path before and made a success of their business. Saving time can also mean outsourcing repetitive activities like using a virtual assistant or buying help at a cheaper hourly rate than your own charge out rate.

Of course, there are other reasons people buy like:

- to feel better (e.g. massage or life coaching)
- to fix a relationship (e.g. counselling or leadership training)
- to live life to the max - (e.g. buying 'experiences')

The more of these 'buying reasons' you can uncover from your prospect and that you cover with your offer, the more likely you are to sell it.

Maybe you have a fast-track solution to a problem. Perhaps you have a blueprint for others to follow that can provide a faster solution by guiding them along a path you have already trodden so that they are less likely to experience the same pitfalls that you did.

Look again at your answers to the Discover your Zone of Genius exercise in online resources, most specifically unpacking your significant life experiences. Do any of them particularly stand out to you? Could you talk about one of them in depth for an hour or more without drying up?

However, be careful not to define all your experiences as qualifying you as 'expert'. Most of them you will have achieved competency but not expertise in. By grouping them all together it muddies the water when you are searching for that one outstanding gift that you can give the world with an expert's eye.

Remember people do not want to pay to hear chapter and verse about you and your experiences. They are looking for the missing information to fix their problem and make their business successful. Give a brief example to back up what you are saying, keep things on point, avoid digressing as at best this will confuse your audience or at worst it will irritate them. I recommend that you give relevant examples but stop short of waffling!

MAKING THE CHOICE

You may have got several business ideas or opportunities in mind to pursue and you're asking yourself '"which one is best?"' or '"what am I really qualified to talk about?"' Indeed, you could already have a business but it just doesn't feel quite 'you'.

Maybe you possibly have blamed an inability to sell as the reason you are not as successful as you had hoped, but what if the real reason is that you need to change direction or at least navigate to a slightly different destination?

Creative thinking is an essential part of growing your business from grass shoots or as you really begin to scale. Always be open to ideas to test.

Whether you are starting out in business or if you've reached 6 figures or above, what I do know is that there is a real magic to thinking big.

It all starts with a vision that you have; perhaps a long held dream that you can now really begin to see how all the moving parts work together. Some people feel this early in life as their destiny. Others start in one occupation, then realise they are destined for another. Then there are people who are constantly flitting from one idea to the next, never settling. It is for these reasons you need to put in the work to find the answers, uncover the missing information and begin to move forward with a driven purpose. If you are really serious about developing a business, then this is a priority. How can you expect to build a house on no foundations?

Listen to your heart. Your heart energy is extremely smart. It gives you a conduit to your gut feeling and intuition.

As Albert Einstein famously said…

"I think 99 times and find nothing. I stop thinking, swim in silence and the truth comes to me".

When you sell from a place of loving what you do, your natural enthusiasm and confidence will shine through. As I've mentioned in earlier chapters, don't worry about what will make you the most money, that will follow if you love what you do.

What you choose to sell will evolve as well as the way you will sell it. Where you start out is unlikely to be the final destination... FACT. This is all part of the fine tuning required as you begin to focus on your genius. Go with the flow and trust your intuition.

So, let's start to narrow things down.

We need to discover which one of your life's experiences you feel the most connected to, the most passionate about, the most confident to talk about anytime, any place, and anywhere. Ask a couple of your good friends what they believe you have to offer the world; what they would come to you for advice or help with. This can be a surprisingly revealing exercise (at least it was for me). Often others see what we don't see ourselves. Our gift comes easily to us, that is why it's so difficult for us to spot! Try it.

CHAPTER 3

Our minds are powerful and when it comes to sales, one of the biggest challenges that women often face is their own mindset. Whether it's believing we're not good enough or dealing with negative thoughts, it's important to work on our mindsets before jumping into sales so that we're ready to handle anything.

This essentially boils down to 5 topics to get clarity on:

1. VALUES

Now that you have looked at your life experiences and started to discover your zone of genius, you may have also noticed similarities in what's been important to you on your journey. Whether it's family, money, certainty, growth or anything else that you see of high importance, these are known as your core values.

And in order to sell and build a profitable business, it's important to know your core values to be able to develop your business' ethos. As a leader, it's important to set expectations so that as your business grows, new people joining will adopt the same values to work to when representing your business. Your list of values will drive your decision making process across your business and will form how you like to sell to your customers.

This can present an issue, because many people are predisposed to adopt the values they were raised with which they naturally believe to be 'right'. So it is very helpful to have a clear view on what the values of your business are, so that you can communicate them effectively. This could literally involve displaying them on the wall or include them within your training manual (if you have one). Your business values represent who you are as a business today, not where you want to be. They represent who you want in your business and who <u>does not belong</u> in your business.

So, let's drill down into a bit more detail to help you uncover what your own business values are.

To give you a little inspiration, answer the following questions:

<u>Who do you most admire in life and what is it about them that you admire</u>?

It may be a friend who has overcome tremendous health challenges and displayed incredible fortitude.

It may be a person who has acquired a wealth of knowledge whilst retaining humbleness.

In my case, my number 1 is my Mum who sees the best in everyone and everything.

<u>What have been some of your best experiences in business</u>?

Did you become a top 3 supplier to a global brand?

Did you find a job for someone who was really struggling in life?

Have you created what quickly became a fast moving, runaway success product?

<u>What have been some of your worst experiences in business</u>?

Have you realised you changed a job too fast without considering what could be the downside and then living to regret the move?

Are you stuck in boring, repetitive work where the day seemed endless and you were clock watching all the time?

Is it your lack of sales conversions?

Is it not knowing how to fix the challenges in your business?

Now review your answers and ask yourself:

What values, traits or attributes was I tapping into when I created the best experiences?

Trust me, ALL of the above have been true for me at one time or another. Good or bad, they served to shape me, my business and my friendships because they became part of me and my values.

Now it's time to create your value statements by honing in on your values. You can access this exercise in the Online Resources area at www.suziseddon.com/resources

Your value statements act as a guide to you making decisions, taking on new clients, recruiting new team members and of course, how you interact in a sales situation, so this is an important exercise to complete.

2. BELIEFS

We all have beliefs and they drive how we think, act and make decisions.

Beliefs are what we believe is true or real that shape our perceptions and actions. That's the surface level answer.

When we look under the surface, the truth is that beliefs guard our mind to keep us safe. Throughout our lives we have built our own Belief Bank so that when we encounter a situation, we reference back to our Belief Bank for what to do next. We take actions based on our belief about a situation and so the result is pretty predictable each time, unless we challenge that belief by checking in to see if it's still true. We all use beliefs as a filter through which we allow things in, or shut them out.

And the words within our beliefs have real power. For example, we've probably all heard this sentence:

'money is the root of all evil'

but the actual original saying was:

'the love of money is the root of all evil'

This is a great example of how beliefs can be influenced or changed by the language used…. in an instant!

Personally, I go with:

MONEY GIVES YOU CHOICES

When we are selling, we really need to learn to extract ALL the different outcomes there could be from a situation we are facing, before jumping to one specifically.

We are all conditioned to think that it is outside events, or people and what they say, that dictate how we feel – but actually it's your own mind that decides that.

So, let me ask you…

Do you believe your prospects can afford your solution?

It is easy to judge a person's ability to pay as soon as you set eyes on them, so just follow the process of opening up dialogue and rapport with open questions before you begin assuming and fall into quick judgement.

As a woman, you know how quickly we read the energy of others but don't forget, they'll be reading yours too! Your certainty is critical to them trusting that you have the answer they are searching for and thus if you can be trusted with their money. Knowing your subject and getting clear on the various permutations of your offer are as important as adopting a mindset of service when creating belief in yourself. Practice phrases that empower you rather than put you in fear of the selling process. A phrase with a clear outcome in mind and a specific reason to call, will position you in the best mindset for a cold call or any sales conversation. The same is true when meeting face to face. Always have a question ready that is linked to the outcome, for example:

"Would you like to know the 3 easy steps to solving behavioural problems with your dog?"

"Would it be helpful to learn the 5 hidden mindsets that sabotage sales success"?

"Would you like to know 5 nutrition hacks that can get you more energy with your thyroid disease?"

"Do you know the 5 top secrets to looking like a pro the next time you are wine-tasting?"

"Do you know the 3 things you can do before going out, to attract and keep a quality man?"

Just a few examples to whet your appetite for creating one or two yourself related to your business area.

Now it's your turn.

Firstly, let's work on your self-beliefs:

What is the most helpful thought you could have before you go into a sales conversation?

And now consider your prospects beliefs:

What is an empowering statement you could say to put your prospect in the most positive energy to buy?

When you take your prospect to their vision and they can see it and feel where they are going, everything makes sense and their fears will move aside.

If you cannot demonstrate that you have belief in yourself and what you offer, don't expect anyone else to. It's a hard truth but it's one that you can navigate by finding those empowering statements and having them ready in your back pocket to lean on when you need them.

3. IMPOSTER SYNDROME

As soon as we start to find our feet and begin to realise that we actually know quite a lot about what we do, you can guarantee that this is the time when the monkey on your shoulder starts whispering in your ear.

"Am I good enough? Do I know enough?"

"Do I offer a unique product/service?"

"Is anyone going to buy it?"

"Will people laugh at me?"

"Am I too old to start something new at my age?"

These thoughts are often signals of our beliefs coming through again, this time the beliefs of ourselves known as either imposter syndrome or self-doubt. Imposter syndrome is the fear of being exposed as a fraud which, despite us knowing that we're not frauds, it's very easy to doubt ourselves anyway, especially when we're told to show up as the "leading expert".

The constant evolution of our world and societies dictate that no one person can claim to be the world's leading expert on anything because we live in a dynamic, ever-changing world. The scientific discoveries of today will pale into insignificance to the emerging sciences of even the next 20 years.

But you are an expert. You are a unique mix of experiences, knowledge and delivery of the same. That mix is your secret sauce. Your experiences are your credibility for your expertise. So you see, you really are unique in what you offer. No, you are not for everyone but that's a good thing. You are for those who you are speaking directly to through your clear marketing messages, who can clearly see and align with what you stand for.

I was confused for a very long time as to what my purpose was in life. I could do lots of things but I couldn't see the correlation between them. My journey across the lily pads seemed never ending until I sat down and did some deep work to understand how they all connected. I did many of the exercises I have included in this book and I am encouraging you to take time to do these as these very exercises helped me find my purpose. It is your responsibility to do the work, to feel what feels right to you and for you, to put it all together and to recognise what is your purpose and privilege to serve to others. You already know some, if not all, of the pieces you need.

The approach to overcome self-doubt or imposter syndrome is similar to the previous exercise to change your beliefs by challenging whether those beliefs are still true and valid or need to be adjusted or changed entirely.

A word of caution: Seeking the answer externally, by asking others, is dangerous and often results in a mismatch. I wouldn't recommend that. Do the foundational work and get it right even if it means additional work to pivot to something you feel is a closer fit for you. Remember your end game is to have a business you absolutely love, because everything else then flows.

4. NEGATIVITY

As emotional beings, women can dwell on thoughts, especially negative ones. We can go through one difficult situation and the more we think about it, the heavier and heavier it gets and before we know it, we've attracted even more challenges into our lives. This is because emotions coupled with thoughts are incredibly powerful.

I was definitely at the front of the queue on this one. There was a time in my life I experienced a catalogue of disasters that left me at an all time low. I spent years stuck in low energy, not realising I was creating more of the same; in fact a self-fulfilling prophecy!

I used to tell myself 'Don't get into the vortex'; which referred to that dark bottomless hole that sucks you into a maelstrom of untethered negative emotions where you throw in every possible bad thought to make yourself feel even worse.

I realised I had become a real victim.

Over time I became more and more aware of my thoughts and the patterns that I kept running, the stories I kept repeating and I knew I had to think in a different way. It was this self awareness and self regulation that helped me form a coping strategy.

As I said, emotions coupled with thoughts are incredibly powerful and it is exactly this combination with positive emotions and thoughts that supercharges manifestation. Thoughts can work for you, or against you. The choice really is yours. In the world of sales, when fear strikes and you feel disabled to even find a way to enter a sales conversation, this is exactly what is at work.

Sometimes we just power through and just get on with it right?

But thoughts become things and the more we "power through" the more brain power we use and the harder we make it for ourselves.

Instead of powering through, it is far better to develop your own emotional intelligence. To become self aware and self regulate your thoughts. Monitor these and you will recognise when things feel off-kilter enabling you to take action and course correct. It's a really important skill for becoming successful in selling.

The remedy is to put fear aside and replace it with a positive thought and then build up positive emotions behind that thought. Doubts, worries and fears are built from thought power and are accelerated when we get emotionally involved.

So you need to be ready to immediately shift your attention toward your dreams and goals, backed with strong emotion, vision and conviction.

Imagine you are aiming to capture the business of a prospect you've had your eye on for a long time. Think of how you are going to approach them. How will you prepare? What can you take with you to help your pitch? Maybe testimonials or data supporting results you've had with others or even mood boards. Whatever you decide, make sure it adds to what you plan to say.

By placing yourself in the shoes of the prospect, you will begin to see things from their point of view; the challenges and the opportunities.

I have a friend who is a top ranking athlete and he used a very powerful visualisation to get through a difficult time when he was recovering from a very serious operation. He is a cyclist and while he couldn't cycle, rather than staying at home and feeling sorry for himself, he would run whole stages of the race like he was riding it for real. Feeling the air on his face, the wind against his body, the smell and the sounds of the countryside. Checking his spot times… the whole thing. The powerful thing about this visualisation was that he felt like it was happening for real so when he did get back on his bike he knew that course like the back of his hand.

Now it's your turn.

Consider now a forthcoming situation where you find yourself a little unsure about how to approach it. Write out your fear and then replace it with as many visions and feelings as you can muster to imagine what it would be like going really well and how you will feel. This will also help you to come up with ideas on how to approach the situation

As women, we are often considered experts with feeling our emotions. It is this skill we must lasso if we find ourselves feeling nervous, perhaps in a meeting or business presentation, by shifting to positive thoughts and most importantly attaching a rich tapestry of emotions to them with all their textures, colours, images, sounds, feelings and even tastes if relevant. This really is one of our superpowers as women. Emotions can often come easily to us, so let's use them!

Supercharge your emotions behind your positive thoughts, then repeat… until the goal is achieved.

Our hearts think for us, with thoughts our minds create for us.

5. PROGRESSIVE THINKING

Progressive thinking is one of the most important skills you can master in life because it enables you to intervene directly into the workings of your mind, to consciously take control of this process so that you choose what things mean and thus how you feel, rather than letting your unconscious mind run away with you and make it mean something that really doesn't play for you.

As women, I believe we can be more sensitive to react negatively in these situations simply because we feel more acutely than guys in the main. So we need to train ourselves to recognise we are beginning to be dragged into the vortex, in order to take action to pull out.

Think about how you react to losing a big sale.

How did you feel about it?
What did you conclude was the problem?
Did it turn out this wasn't the problem?

Think about criticism you've received from someone.

How did you feel about it?
Did you unpack all the possible reasons why they felt their criticism was valid?
Did you ask them!?

Probably not and this is often the time we reach inside for reference and blame ourselves.

Think about something new you've tried and it was a complete and utter failure.

What did that mean to you?
What meaning did you attach to it?

These are the times we need to take a moment to revisit our range of beliefs and check-in as to whether they are still valid.

Mini Exercise

1. Run through some situations now that have upset, frustrated or annoyed you.
2. What meaning did you attach to why this situation happened?
3. List 3 meanings that you **could** have associated with this – play out all three in your mind and note how your perception of the situation changes.

MASTER YOUR MINDSET

CHAPTER 4

LETTING GO

As women, it's very common to feel as though, over time, in personal relationships, we may have started to feel we are losing our identity. After all, many of us carry the label of somebody's Mother or somebody's Wife or Partner, rather than our own job title per se.

We give away fragments of ourselves to our relationships, our families, our children and it is our nurturing and care we give of freely and abundantly to the long queue forming at the door to take, take, take. Soon we can lose sight of ourselves, putting others before us and suddenly we don't know who we are, what we stand for, or our life's purpose. We have subjugated ourselves to last on the list with others taking our good heart for granted.

Sound familiar?

All of our experiences in life move us toward understanding what our contribution is to the world. Rather annoyingly of course, this unfurls over time. Life prefers to prepare us one step on the lily pad at a time. Each step revealed along the way. When I look back at my own journey, I now understand how I got here. Simply put, my mess became my message. Some life experiences can have a profound effect on us like massive tectonic plates shifting our consciousness and it can be very uncomfortable. Sometimes this leaves us with more questions than answers as we struggle to stabilise. It becomes part of our life story as we keep replaying it over and over again. Every time we repeat it, it becomes more ingrained into our soul. This was me. I couldn't make sense of what was happening to me so I kept replaying the same mind movie again and again in the hope of finding the missing information.

At any given moment we are all in choice. We can choose to move beyond, or we can choose to stay stuck. By <u>not</u> choosing to move forward we essentially self-select to stay stuck. At this point a vortex of negativity increases in strength and begins to whir around you until you feel overwhelmed, demotivated, confused, worried and maybe even helpless. This is when the power of friendship and guidance really counts to regain perspective, to gain new insights to coax you to move forward. In my business, I find that with my coaching clients this is very often the time when people move toward me for help, to get unstuck and to finally make progress and to realise their dream.

Letting go and moving on can be so difficult. Difficulties happen in all areas of life and some people deal with them better than others. Heart led individuals can really struggle, particularly if they are heart led souls with a core of feminine energy. I believe it's connected to a feeling of failure, which is tied to the nurturing piece within us that demands we always show up and never give up. In truth if something isn't working (a business idea, a relationship, a project you've worked so hard on that won't seem to take off) the smartest thing you can do is to move away from it and put your precious energy into something else that gives you a return financially, morally and spiritually. Whether it's a business idea, a relationship or a project you've worked so hard on that won't seem to take off, when it's not working, it's time to let it go. When something isn't a strain and you aren't struggling to make ends meet and you are in flow, this is when the magic ignites. This is at the root of the law of attraction.

So how do you let go?

Well as George Bernard Shaw said "those who cannot change their minds cannot change anything".

Or as Tony Robbins put it…"by changing nothing, nothing changes"

Notice the patterns in your life, then look to alter them.

Change your routine, change the type of information you consume and the media you consume it from.

Expand your thinking by introducing new skills or meeting new groups of people. Notice the patterns in your life, then look to alter them. Some of these changes will result in an injection of new energy within you. New ideas will come from introductions to new people.

SOUL SISTERS

Many people start things but don't think about what they need around them and more importantly, who you need around you.

People around us can become very judgemental as we begin to change and venture into new avenues. Some tell us what we are trying to achieve is above us; that maybe we are better than we think we are. They tell us to get a normal job.

In the main this comes from a place of care but it also comes through the only lens they have – their own. Their own experiences or hearing about others who have had negative or difficult experiences trying to achieve the same. What becomes clear is that they don't have the same driving force or conviction we possess as entrepreneurs. They want the safest option and for some this means sticking with their humdrum life of predictability, being pay-rolled by someone else who sings the tune for them to dance to. Independent business owners and entrepreneurs are seeking real opportunity to gain their time and money freedom and/or other objectives at a faster pace and claiming more of the rewards for their labour, than just getting a monthly pay cheque signed off by someone else, who coincidentally *is* an entrepreneur.

Sadder still are those who not only judge you when you are digging deep for treasure but also when you are buzzing with excitement for the project you are working on or even worse when you begin to taste success. They hang on to any hiccup they perceive along the way, whilst often not acknowledging the forward momentum you are creating.

Yes, many people do this.

Most of them are family and friends but can even be a spouse who believes they are giving you the best advice - but in truth unless you have your hand up for help, it only serves to irritate because it is not a path they would ever take or even understand why you would. This is why the early phases of entrepreneurship can be a challenge because, in addition to the steep learning curve, you are very likely having to navigate the negativity of others on an ongoing basis, even when success arrives at your door.

This is why it is so very important to build a group of like-minded individuals around you, soul sisters if you like, who share not only your values, your drivers and your journey but also your struggles and successes too. It is so important to surround yourself with 'can do' people and not those who often say you 'can't do X because of Y...'.

Choose carefully and stick to those who are treading the same road of entrepreneurship. You will learn much from them as well as receiving support when you need chivvying up and celebration as you tick off your milestones.

So where do you find them?

In part, this depends on the type of business you have. Whether you are in retail, product development or the service industry, you probably attend shows and events where you are likely to meet like-minded stallholders or speakers. Then there are masterminds or other training sessions and of course online groups and workshops that can help you open dialogue with others whom you gel with. There is something very comforting in forming a bond with others facing the same challenges, to exchange ideas and to help you think through options and solutions.

Write a list of 3 communities online or locally where your own sisterhood group exists and think about how you can nurture your relationships with them.

This is the importance of finding like-minded women in business so that we can support each other on our respective journeys and importantly we don't lean on our families and friends, asking for advice or direction they may be ill equipped to give.

At every level, friendship feeds the mental well-being of a woman as well as supporting us on the path to success. You just need to open up and raise your hand for help if you need it.

BUILD RELATIONSHIPS

What type of business are you in?

I'll tell you... "it's the relationship business, not the transaction business" (a great quote from Dan Kennedy). Again, this is a throwback to the 1980's and 90's, where it was all about closing business in your black suit and white shirt and nothing at all about building connection. At that time Business Managers placed the onus on "getting the sale" rather than in tandem, nurturing relationships for future sales.

Repeat business is so valuable as going forward it represents the lowest hanging fruit, meaning it's the easiest to get, to gain more sales, faster, from an already warm customer. In fact, I will go one step further and suggest that right here, right now as you read this, I bet you can find some repeat business you are potentially about to leave on the table. We all do it.

So, the key is to build strong relationships with your customers and look after them. Perhaps you could give them VIP status with advanced priority to up and coming new products, services or events you are running? This could nurture these people into becoming not just customers but your raving fans who will then go on to sing your praises from the hilltops.

Today we have a plethora of tools and software that drill into our data. In essence this is how we all suddenly realised we had a lot of repeat customers. At one time they would have slipped unnoticed under the radar, simply because the data mining tools weren't available. Repeat customers are a prized asset for any business, especially today and that is why it is so important to keep connection to them.

When I analyse my past successes in sales, all have been gained through me fostering great relationships and rapport first but then continuing to keep in touch after the sale. People love that you stay connected. Actually, I love it too because I carefully selected my right fit buyers. They are people I enjoy spending time with, and this is one of the keys to success.

As a society we now have less human connection on a day-to-day basis than ever. We don't go out as much, we join fewer clubs, we have less time to spend with family and friends and all because the world of tech took over. Most particularly I am talking about Zoom and similar platforms. We sacrificed face-to-face relationships and substituted technology as a time saving tool at the expense of not witnessing the same energy 'in-person'. It is also now why so many people have moved back to attending in-person events given the choice to attend online or in real life. Let's face it, we are all social beings. There is no substitute for being in front of someone. It is far easier to read body language and to hear changes in voice modulation and context.

Much of your personal power and thus your impact is stolen by computers so please make a 'Note to Self' to get in front of your prospects and customers as much and as often as possible.

I often get asked what to do at a networking event if someone seems interested in what you do and how to elegantly move towards the sales conversation. The truth is that networking meetings are a great opportunity to use your 15-word descriptor when you are asked about what you do. It is the softly, softly approach to spreading the word about your business. Watch for the response. If they are interested they will likely self-select to receive more information. Not everyone is going to be a right fit as a prospective client so leave the gap for them to step into after giving the information and don't keep pushing if they are less than enthusiastic.

CREATE YOUR TOP PROSPECTS LIST

Make a list of your top 20 prospects, follow them on social media, noting their interests and likes so that you can, if appropriate, at some point send them a surprise gift they will love.

This will help to build the relationship and warm up a potential customer.

CHAPTER 5

GRABBING ATTENTION

In sales, whether you're just starting out or have been doing it for a while, it can be easy to get lost for words especially when it comes to describing ourselves and what we offer. It's one of those things that gets pushed to the bottom of the list, when it needs to be at the top!

If you're just starting out, I know things can seem so overwhelming at the beginning with so much to do but this exercise is important not just to get clarity for yourself but also for your prospects who need a concise description of what your business can offer them in a few words. Most business owners that don't prepare this end up waffling on at this point, trying to convince or explain, which as we know is a big mistake.

If you're an established business, this is a very worthwhile exercise for you too.

As we can all appreciate, often the customer we work with can change as our business evolves, and as we grow and scale our businesses we most likely move to a different type of customer. We therefore need to recalibrate and refocus on how we grab attention.

The first piece any business entrepreneur needs to master is to grab attention, to confidently deal with new enquiries, to attend networking events with a succinct description about what you do. This will draw interest from people who are searching madly for your guidance and will ensure you are no longer at a loss for words to capture that audience.

The goal here is to create a 15-word statement known as your "Descriptor". This is a statement that describes who you help and what you help them achieve.

To make it really easy and straightforward, I'll be providing a fill-in-the-blanks document for you to complete and you'll learn why niching and micro-niching is really important when defining your audience.

You can download it now from www.suziseddon.com/resources

Now this is where things get interesting.

Armed with your new Descriptor, it's now time to try it on for size! In other words, see how it feels.

Is it easy to say?

Does it trip off your tongue?

Use your smartphone to record yourself saying it and feel how it is to receive those words by re-playing to yourself.

It may differ from what you have been saying to date, but now you have done a little more work and have become clearer on your life experiences, skills, likes, dislikes, passions, where your enthusiasm sits in relation to what you do as a business and the mission you want to accomplish, you will be much clearer when speaking about what you do to a stranger.

And it is very likely you will create many versions of this as you drill down into what you do and what you *want* to do.

For example, mine started as:

"I coach women to sell with confidence using a feminine energy sales process".

Many iterations and lots of tweaking later, I settled on:

I coach women in business 45+ how to have easy sales conversations that convert to clients, without sounding pushy and manipulative.

Also, don't be surprised if you find you have changed the topic entirely. The important thing is for you to be settled with it and that it feels right as you begin to use it in public to a stranger. This could be at a networking event or simply when you are out at dinner and someone asks "what do you do in life?"

Deciding on your descriptor is likely to take some work and you will no doubt tweak it over time until it feels right and you can speak it out with ease and confidence. Don't forget that as your business changes or expands, this needs to be reflected in your descriptor.

The purpose of your descriptor is to ascertain top line interest. In other words, if it receives a positive reaction like "'oh tell me more'" or whether it is met with glazed eyes. Either is great. You, or what you do, will not appeal to everyone so keep your expectations in check. At best you could be about to enter your first or next sales conversation, at worst the other person will smile and acknowledge the information. If the descriptor is really good, then that person will have the same nugget to feed to a possible lead for you. That is why it's so valuable.

Take your time, mull things over and don't expect to have it figured out in the next 10 minutes. Test it with friends. Shockingly many of your friends are probably still unclear on what you do. Ask them, then test, test, test your new descriptor. See what feels right and most importantly what communicates clearly and concisely what your business is about to people.

THE POWER OF STORY

A positive mindset fosters a positive vibration. This is an important state to be in because it is exactly what you will exude to a prospect.

You may need a bit of extra help to get into that confident mindset before beginning the call and this is when we can use the power of telling a story ready in our back pocket to help us.

Whether we are doing a video or we are talking face to face with a prospect, we need to be thinking in terms of creating a pattern interrupt; being a way to stop a prospect in their tracks before they lose interest and/or close us down.

To do this we need to feel good about ourselves. Strangely this is often quite difficult to do. It's not so easy to 'blow one's own trumpet'. However, a very effective way of doing it is to tell a story. For example, it could be a story about when you have been a key part in someone else's transformation journey.

However, if you are starting out in business, you may be thinking that you haven't actually been paid by anyone yet for such advice, so how are you going to prove your value? That you haven't been paid for your expertise yet doesn't matter. In fact, it's irrelevant because what people are really interested in is understanding how you made a measurable difference. In other words, the transformation you played a valuable part in effecting.

For example, years ago I was doing some charity work and I coached an ex-convict. He had done a long stretch at Her Majesty's prison and he came out to a totally different world that he just wasn't equipped to deal with. Worse still, no one would employ him for a decent wage and for a number of years he had been on half of what was deemed the Basic Wage by the Government at the time (£5.50 per hour). One day he joked that he was really good at foot massage and I joked back saying "then why don't you get paid for it and moreover, why don't you start a foot massage business!" Obviously, this was met with a fair amount of disdain. I pointed out that he really did have limited options given his chequered past but that this opportunity could really fly for him. With my help, he created some high-quality business cards with an image of a woman's feet in a daisy field. He completely flipped out when I told him the going rate for this service was £40 per hour and we had to do some work together on his beliefs around money, for him to be comfortable enough to believe he was worth this and to say it with confidence.

Wherever he goes in the world now, he can take his work in his backpack, with creams and foot files, and receipt book. He also now has a job that he can ably do later into life to compensate for the lack of income earlier and of course when the time comes to slow down, he can adapt his days accordingly. He is now back in his power.

Today he has a thriving business, and I couldn't be prouder of him.

This is an example of a story I could tell to emphasise how I support my clients with their mindset.

Let people hear about the value of investing in you by sharing a story. Let them into the emotion and energy you give out. Let them vicariously feel what that transformation journey is like. This is the way you attract your ideal clients by being real, being vulnerable and creating an energetic bubble of trust and opportunity around you for prospects to choose to walk into. This is not about putting yourself on a pedestal to be admired. It's about pulling together the threads of your experience and creating a real-life opportunity to showcase what you offer.

As always, it's not about you, it's about them, their transformation journey and putting their needs first. Resist the opportunity to get caught up re-living the high emotion of the story because then it becomes about you.

Avoid using in depth, lengthy examples from your own life. Keep stories relevant and succinct to what your audience is seeking.

The power of story is all around us, most particularly in the world of film and television and this is why we are all so partial to a story because it takes us on an emotional journey.

Can you remember a time when someone asked for your input and the help you gave changed the course of what they do today?

Now craft a succinct story around it, ready to deliver to your own audience.

DON'T GET IT PERFECT, GET IT DONE

CHAPTER 6

MAGNETICALLY ATTRACT EXACTLY WHO YOU WANT TO WORK WITH

All life is energy.

You may be lucky enough to know that feeling of meeting someone for the first time when two souls recognise each other at a deep level. As youngsters, we were much better at going with the flow, tuning in and listening to our inner voice but as we got older, we became less trusting of our instincts. We began letting our minds dictate to us, convincing ourselves to make decisions against our gut instinct or worse still letting others convince us, even though we already had a developed inner knowing.

As can now be appreciated, personal vibration really counts for numerous reasons, especially with regard to the world of frequencies helping you to identify the ideal person you want to work with, known as your Right Fit Customer.

Think about this for a moment.... As youngsters we recognised that we did not want everyone in the playground as a friend. So why in business do we try to persuade everyone to do business with us?

Influence and serve customers in their quest for a solution to their pain or challenge but don't persuade. Persuading feels pushy and manipulative and is diametrically opposed to serving and selling with ease.

For these reasons, it is imperative to have a very clear idea of who you want as a customer. People get confused quickly if you are not really clear about who you want to attract to work with. Then you get super disappointed when your offers fall flat and no one buys, or even worse when later on, buyers realise you do not fit what they were looking for and request a refund.

It's much better for us to get really clear on who we are, what we have to offer and then craft an irresistible offer to attract those madly searching the internet to find us! Sometimes this is referred to as niching or micro niching or identifying your right fit customer. It is just a huge mistake to throw your offers open to a broad audience or worse still everyone, like trying to hold a handful of sand tightly and then watching helplessly as the grains of sand escape through your fingers.

We need to be aiming to market to a specific set of individuals, with a super clear message. In this way we become known as a stand-out contributor in our field or yes even as the expert.

Understanding exactly who your right fit audience is, is imperative to your success in business. None of us appeal to everyone. In fact, we really need to slim down the funnel to hone in tightly to appeal to a subset group.

So, who is your right fit audience?

Have you noticed if they share commonalities?

Are they in the same age group?

Are they Professional people?

Do they share similar interests?

Are they family oriented?

You can access the Right Fit Audience exercise in the Online Resources area at www.suziseddon.com/resources

AUDIENCE MAKEUP

It's very easy to get into a flat spin when it comes to keeping everything up in the air. As women this isn't just about our business, it includes partners, family, children, house, elderly relations and the list goes on. Social media has become an important element of sales so we need to become super organised, not least disciplined, to keep on top of it. This, of course, starts with understanding who your audience are. Your audience will in turn be made up of different styles of buyers:

Emotional buyers, who make decisions quickly based on their gut feeling.

When think of something or a situation, our thinking is made up of:

(1) pictures in our mind's eye

(2) the internal dialogue we play

(3) the sounds we hear.

That is why one of the best tips for Flow State Selling is to understand that if you can hit all 3, this can result in naturally closing a sale and is far easier than you having to 'close the sale' per se.

Logical buyers, who are data driven, need all the questions answered before they feel able to make a decision.

Visuals, who prefer to visualise an image or graphic and tend to love social media.

Auditory people, who prefer real life conversations and obviously podcasts.

Kinesthetics, who love a task or a problem to solve and need interesting content to mix things up.

And lastly Readers who represent the highest percentage and probably include you and me and are already abundantly served by all the printed or written material out there.

Which category do you fit into?

Big picture strategist, blue-sky thinker or data driven diva - your potential buyers could also be a real mix.

When you start to compare and contrast this question across a variety of people you know, you will understand that your content needs to be rich enough to satisfy the wide variety of potential buyers out there, whilst maintaining a clear marketing message that will motivate them to self-select 'in' or 'out' for your offer.

As important, is that you put out the same consistent message and brand across all your marketing and social channels because every step a prospect takes toward you, they are checking and rechecking that you really do have the solution they are searching for.

So, there is real value in appealing across the spectrum of learning styles when communicating information from the first touch your audience experiences with you, right through to when you make offers to them and beyond when they become a valued customer and later raving fans if you continue to serve their needs.

Maintaining 'high touch' with lots of interaction in the early days of a new relationship is the best way to nurture newbies who will have a high degree of thirst for information to fix the challenge they are hoping you will provide.

Once you have gained some traction and prospects have started to move towards you like responding to emails, downloading a pdf from you, registering for a workshop or webinar, the next is very likely a sales conversation.

CHAPTER 7

Now that we've covered grabbing attention and understanding your audience's makeup, it's time to consider where you run your business and how you can bring your customers together.

ONLINE, OFFLINE OR BOTH?

How do you feel when you think about taking your business online or even your online business offline?

Sometimes the old and the new world collide. The traditional way of selling meets the new, online-kid-on-the-block and as a business owner, you need to decide if it's appropriate to have a presence in one or both.

There is no doubt it is always good to understand how each could affect you, your business and especially your competitors. It doesn't mean that you have to follow suit but it is smart to see how this could change the playing field by viewing things from another perspective. Be aware of what's going on in the world, but don't necessarily jump in or let it drive your decisions. Choose to manage your own stage – BE AWARE BUT NOT ABSORBED.

COMMUNITY SPIRIT

Engaged communities are really valuable to us in business.

People used to think nothing about turning out on a foggy autumn evening for a meeting but then the world changed and with it we all adapted to meeting online.

Zoom and other platforms arrived and whilst not perfect, as time has passed, it has given us the 'virtual live event'; a different kind of experience but one that has been proved to have the ability to create a community that feels driven to stick together long after the event is over.

It has enabled professionals to consult with clients and patients, chefs to teach online and schools to educate in online classes. It has also enabled the solopreneur to compete against the big boys and girls of the business world and for that, I for one, am truly thankful.

So, I have a question for you:

Are your competitors finding new ways to sneak in through the back door of your business?

It's definitely worth asking yourself this question.

For the vast majority of businesses, it has been possible to supplement a real life method with an online version, giving a whole new experience. I am quite sure this will never replace real life interaction - there is no substitute for that - but for times in our lives when time is short, when we are unwell at home or when it is actually a foggy autumn evening, then Zoom and similar platforms have proved to be an invaluable addition to help us get things done.

When we walk into a room, we feel the energy of that room. It's palpable both in the positive or the negative. This is often exaggerated at a large gathering or event where you can feel a groundswell of excitement building. It's why people love going to the theatre or to see a band Live on stage. You not only feel connected with whoever is on stage, you also feel very connected to the people around you whose high energy will rub off on you too, creating an electric atmosphere which is hard to beat.

Many years ago, I used to sell at country fairs and I had a stall. I loved meeting such a variety of people and how every space I entered, be it in a massive marquee, a town hall or a field, I just loved the setup which was unique to the space. It gave me a theme to play with, giving me an endless supply of inspiration for my personal creativity. I loved it. My energy for this was always high and do you know what? You could tell. Serving your people and making an effort to stand out from the crowd really works. Today we use the term in social media about 'stopping the scroll' well this is how to do it in the real world. I was always busy. I created a look which was visually arresting, that stopped shoppers in their tracks, that gave them ideas and inspiration in their buying choices. Other stallholders who just went through the motions of setting up the same stall set-up, time and time again, projected little or no energy to attract new browsers and buyers and their lack of sales was written all over their grumpy faces. The point I am trying to make is that there really is no substitute for real life interaction. In this example, if it is coupled with the ability to bring people into a buzzy community event where you can discuss your product 1:1 and the prospective customers can touch it or even hear it, then that is the holy grail of how to sell with ease.

Sam Walton of Wal-Mart fame was a great believer in service to his employees, customers and the wider communities that supported his business because he believed that if he looked after people, they would look after him. Service to all was his 'why' in business. That is why you need to be bothered to serve your customers at the highest level.

RUNNING EVENTS

If your business involves training, coaching or consulting, perhaps running an event could be a great strategy for you to bring it all together.

This could be an in-person event, a webinar, a summit, a challenge or any other ideas that you have to bring a community together.

When organising events, it's important to create a rich mixture of content, information, imagery, guests etc and market it effectively. This will probably cross the online/offline world divide by using both printed media and social media for promotion.

As an online event organiser, it's key to energise the whole experience of the event by using props, encouraging audience participation such as singing, setting tasks, breakout rooms and inviting guest speakers. In this way the audience co-creates the energy of the event, rather than being a passive entrant, observer/listener. Fundamentally understand the co-creation piece and you'll win in this space.

In an offline event, many people talk about the real-life networking opportunities enjoyed as a result of being together. It is often held as one of the best outcomes of in-person events.

For an online event the audience often does not want to leave behind the new community they have just become part of at the end of the event. The camaraderie built is a big driver for taking up any offer to buy products, programmes or services because people want the opportunity to continue their journey both by learning together and to get "back in the room" together.

Online challenges are another great example of a virtual live event that has taken the online world by storm. Challenges are events run usually between 5-30 days, where one key piece of information a day is revealed to registrants toward the promise you have made at the outset. For example, I have a 10X Your Leads Challenge, where I teach people over 5 days, a method of finding lots of relevant leads for their business, with no monetary cost. Typically, I make an offer during the challenge giving participants the opportunity to sign up to my Immersion Program and thus continue their journey with the same people on the same path, who they have just begun to get to know.

> **Top Tip:**
>
> There is no doubt that with any online event, computers steal energy. I first experienced this about 15 years ago when I was recording an audio series. I honestly thought I was projecting my voice really well down the microphone until I listened back to the recording. It was lacklustre, almost monotone. I had to re-record it and use far more energy, enunciation, projection and tonality for my message to land with my listener. Without doing so it was simply flat and boring.
>
> This is why it is so important to meet and see as many of your prospects and customers 'in person' as possible, especially when growing your business because there is no real substitute for real-life interaction.

ENGAGE THEIR SENSES

When reaching out to any audience, whether it be online or offline, offer a rich experience by tapping into as many senses as possible to engage your audience.

For this reason, it has become popular in recent years to send out a physical goody box ahead of an online event that contains a number of props such as door hangers, water bottles, wipeable charts and pens, stickers and emoji paddles to use during the event. Indeed, I do the same for some of my larger events, including my special Halloween events, complete with spooky masks, face paint, stickers and I even provide a special Zoom background. People love receiving goody boxes and speaking as the person often in front of the camera, I find it is so much more fun to include props when presenting because it 10X's the energy of the participants because they are not a sedentary listener. They have things to do.

Of course, the goody bag doesn't just live in the online world. Many events, especially in the celebrity world, use them as a way of attracting busy celebrities to their events with expensive goody bags. This time it's where the offline world has moved to the online world.

Great energy is everything, especially in selling but not exclusively in selling. Think of the last time you attended a fitness class and how the energy of the instructor made a huge difference to your participation and/or enjoyment. We often need to be sold to, especially where motivation is concerned.

CHAPTER 8

GLADIATOR HORMONES TO THE RESCUE

When stepping into the spotlight, whether it be selling from behind a counter, on a stage or doing a live event online, most of us feel some level of stress. So as business owners it is important for us to learn about stress, why it happens and how it affects us and how we can deal with it. If you understand what happens to yourself or indeed your customers in a stressful situation, you can manage the situation far better.

The stress factor is interesting because it can change the way we show up. I call this 'wearing the mask'. We suddenly act differently. We use our voices differently, sometimes forced as if to underpin the message we are trying to convey. The difficulty with this is obviously we no longer sound like our natural selves. We present like our AI version, sounding a little strangled and definitely unnatural. Simply put, we are now sending out mixed messages because we have lost our centre.

So, what happens inside our bodies at these moments?

In practice, the body reacts swiftly to live interaction by firing up a range of hormones whilst it 'reads' a situation, assessing and re-calibrating itself on the fly. We enjoy a dose of Oxytocin when we meet friends, particularly when we are intimate, but the moment we sense danger Cortisol, the fight or flight hormone, immediately floods our system so we can react with lightning fast focus. This heady mix of a variety of what I call 'gladiator' hormones, are released in different quantities depending on the situation in which we find ourselves. The body is an amazing computer in and of itself.

It is for this reason that the situations we place ourselves in like selling from behind a counter, in front of a camera, on audio, online or on a stage will subconsciously be communicating with our body whilst at the same time, liaising with our hormone system for support.

Understanding stress responses can really help you grasp what is going on, not only within yourself but also with your prospects and customers. As we grow and change as women, we can appreciate our clients do too. So, by being receptive to any stress response you pick up from your prospects and customers, you can also help them navigate it, proving your worth as a trusted extension of their team and not just another salesperson. This ability to listen and express understanding is a feminine energy superpower. After all, we all have a need to be heard, don't we?

When it comes to stress, women typically deal with it through friendships. The old adage, a problem shared is a problem halved, springs to mind. This is our safety release valve. Of course, this is why finding like-minded soul sisters who understand the trials and tribulations of starting, running, growing or scaling a business is very important.

Conversely the stress response in men is that they tend toward the fight or flight or simply bottle up emotions and won't discuss things openly until they have figured out a way forward.

As women our hormone cocktail makeup is so radically different to the guys, is it any wonder why women and men act completely differently in a similar situation?

This is particularly obvious in sales and selling.

BREATHE EASY

When we feel stressed or overcommitted, breathing is the one thing we don't think of as the remedy but we should.

We need to create a different energy within, a gap if you like. If you think about it, many of us breathe very shallowly, a lot of the time. I know I snatch my breath all too often, especially if I am trying to do something complicated like a spreadsheet and I find myself holding my breath. However, I have learned that this has a direct, knock-on effect in my body. Shallow breathing causes anxiety signals in our body and puts our body 'on caution' that something potentially negative is about to occur; that we may have to run or fight imminently. This is another situation where Cortisol comes to our rescue.

For these reasons it's super important to take action and the great news is that you have the power within you to get things back on an even keel.

The good news is that most people can resolve elevated stress largely with breathwork. There are many great books on the subject but essentially, it's about taking time to reconnect with yourself, slow your mind and take it away from all the noise of life for a while. It takes practice. The experts recommend every day for at least 30 days and the results are oh so worth it.

I also use a very simple method of switching from my mind to my ears.

By that I mean I use the sound of my in-breath, and then the sound of my out-breath, to still my mind. Two simple steps.

If you find your mind interfering, just bring your consciousness back to your breathing. It's tremendously effective. I liken it to when steam is released from a pressure cooker; letting go in a slow controlled way.

Sometimes the problem and the solution are right there inside of us.

AUDIT YOUR OWN HAPPINESS

CHAPTER 9

GETTING UNSTUCK & MOVING FORWARD

Our natural feminine energy can sometimes lead us to over analyse but perhaps the roots of this forms through insecurity or not feeling supported. When this plays out in business, we can feel isolated if we are a solopreneur or even if we are not! Women have a propensity to second check ourselves. Many times, we hold back from acting on instinct.

When challenges arise of course we need to analyse what's going on but not to the extent of over analysing. Those little whispers inside you are there for a reason. That's our gut feeling at work. Uncovering a full understanding of the situation by asking questions is the way forward, rather than over-analysing and guessing the answers. Many people come up with 'the answer' off the cuff even though they have little or no information to back it up.

Whenever you find yourself in this situation, stop, ask a few searching questions or even counsel the opinion of others, re-group and then move forward. Don't expect to have all the answers all of the time. Don't put that pressure on yourself. Several heads are better than one.

In all regards, hang on to the good stuff in your life rather than keep processing the bad. It's odd that we all have a knack for doing that! Over analysing keeps you stuck in the past and not creating your future.

Obviously, we can experience horrible things in both our personal and business lives. Sometimes as we process things in background mode, thoughts leak across the barrier and we find something in our personal life is now affecting our business life. I call it cross box contamination!

Whether born out of a personal or business situation, actually feeling our emotions, especially when linked to some bad thing that happened to us, is important because if we suppress them they remain unresolved and embed within us. I took over a decade to learn this lesson. The more I ignored it, the deeper into my subconscious the problem took hold. Years later, it took quite a lot of effort and therapy to 'get at it' as seemingly it forms layers, like sedimentary rock strata, which takes considerably more time to chip through than it did to form!

Sound familiar?

The moral of the story is to feel into the emotion, deal with it and resolve to move on. There's no currency in remaining stuck in the past when you could be creating your future.

So, the next time you are feeling stuck, be quizzical and ask yourself what has led to your feeling this way? Dig deep and ask yourself where you are stuck and if you can't put your finger on it, take your best guess. Now, who do you know who can help you? Perhaps it is someone you know who has faced a similar challenge.

VISUALISE SUCCESS AND PLAN FOR IT

So, what represents success to you? Money? Achievements? Attaining lifelong dreams?

What is your why? Why are you doing the business you have chosen? What is it all for? To buy property, to fund the kids' education, so that you can afford to travel across the globe, or perhaps it is so that you can enjoy retirement without financial worry?

Here's the thing. The more outrageously humongous you build out the detail of your dream, the more likely you are to manifest it by feeling it's so real it already exists in your life!

Think big and design the life you want, today.

I have a dream of having an ocean side property, where I can see dolphins playing offshore every day. It's a big dream and I even have a screenshot of the actual property I want to buy. I have it all mapped out in detail.

Your WHY is not only important in achieving your goals but is your driver when the going gets tough. It will help you to push forward even when things are not going so well. When your business is your life's work and purpose you have a spring in your step every day and a destination in mind.

But to get to it, you have to plan and then swing into action.

Follow these six steps to plan for your success:

1. Write down your yearly goal

2. Write out your quarterly goals that will get you to the yearly goal

3. Write out your month on month goals

4. List what 'stock in trade' you have to sell. It could be a product, a course, an in-person workshop, a discovery day or an online presentation. Make an

exhaustive list. Include any new projects, courses, presentation ideas you want to develop too.

5. Divide your year into 12 points on a horizontal timeline.

6. Decide and place your selections on the timeline, allowing time to create and promote the content.

YOU'VE GOT THIS

CHAPTER 10

AVOIDING BURNOUT & OVERWHELM

Building a business has some incredible benefits but it can also be a long-term drain on your own personal energy if you're not careful, so looking after yourself is a must.

During the COVID19 pandemic in 2020, like many people, I immersed myself in work. I spent far too much time immobile by concentrating on pushing my business forward every day. It was my way of coping whilst living alone.

The problem was that before too long I started living only in my head. I wasn't tapping into my pool of feminine energy and intuition to open up my creativity with a fresh vision.

This is the beginning of getting stuck. Stuck for new ideas, stuck to see clearly and stuck to strategize. Soon overwhelm uncomfortably arrives, when you have racked up so many things in your mind to take action on, but can't quite see where the pieces fit!

Result = No Action.

Keeping yourself in flow internally on a regular basis is of paramount importance.

Take time for self-care, whatever self-care is for you.

- a day by the sea
- a swim
- a spin class
- walking, with or without a dog
- yoga or pilates class
- or just a good massage

Moving built up tension and stress out of your body also serves to loosen your mind. Many people work like mad, then take a week off when they're completely exhausted and for the first few days they sleep their way through the first half of their vacation.

Much better to build in regular self-care activities or what I like to call Flow Maintenance so that the body and mind get used to releasing tension on a regular basis, rather than powering through for days and weeks with no end in sight.

This was my pattern.

With too much Cortisol coursing through my body, the knock-on effect was an acute difficulty sleeping and a massive inability to lose weight also soon arrived at my door to deal with. Not to mention the impact that also had on my business.

Meditation is a relaxation practice that is sometimes regarded as a bit off-the-wall but in my own experience, it has proved to be invaluable. I was taught a very simple method to get into a relaxed meditative state without the worry that you aren't doing it right. The old adage of being told 'just think of nothing' is a stretch too far for most people to grasp.

Similar to what I shared in Chapter 8, the best tip I ever picked up on the subject was to switch from my mind to my ears. By that I mean moving from thinking to listening, most specifically to my in-breath and my out-breath. That was the only instruction given "just listen to your in-breath, then listen to your out-breath and if your mind wanders, switch back to your ears and listen". Next, slow your breathing down and hold your in-breath each time to the count of 5 and then 10 or above if comfortable to do.

This remarkably stills the mind but again, if your mind wanders just become conscious of listening to your breathing again. Twenty minutes is remarkably restorative.

Treat your day like a good exercise class, with points of tension but also release. Your body and mind need a similar fitness program to work optimally. It all starts with planning.

PLANNING TO MANAGE OVERWHELM

Today's woman is a real plate-spinner, juggling the responsibilities of family life, marriage, caregiving to elders, domestic humdrum, cheerleading and yes working too, each element chipping away at our time.

We look back to the time of our grandmother's and realise how much more opportunity we have today to make our own mark on the world now we are not as tied to the home. As a result, we have taken on many more roles.

My own Mother did not return to work until I was 16 years old. When she did, she took a part time job looking after a show home for a local housing developer. In the mid 1970's it was quite unusual for a woman to take a job and was seen very much as just for some 'pin money'.

Years later, when I was married, I used to say to my husband 'I come home to a house, you come home to a home'. By the time he arrived home I had got the logs in, made a fire, fed the dogs, and started making a meal from the food shopping I had done at lunchtime. I had to get the washing under way and fit in the ironing too. I had little time to myself, but I was creating choices for us with the money I earned, like additional holidays, weekends away, private health care and affording smarter clothes.

So, what started as 'pin money' turned into a valuable second household income.

Things had to change, not least, in the way we planned our time. If we don't plan, time runs through our fingers.

Today the internet and social media is awash with apps exploring the most time efficient way to run one's day tying us not to our house this time but to our computers or smartphones.

Time blocking is one strategy that has become very popular which is where you block time out in your calendar for specific times with the blocks referring more to objectives than to a To Do List.

What are your top 3 strategies for managing overwhelm?

Managing your day is one of the best ways to manage overwhelm and to do that we need to schedule. If we don't, we risk reacting to everything that comes front field. Much better to schedule so that we don't get distracted or simply run out of valuable selling time.

Now it's your turn.

Write out the tasks of a typical day for you.

Maybe it involves:

- Planning objectives
- Goal Setting
- Client delivery (or however you deliver your product or service)
- Fitness or exercise
- Household admin
- Business admin
- Food shopping
- Phone calls
- Self-care time
- Food preparation

- Family time
- Thinking and reflection time

Resist being driven by other people's timetables, agendas, needs or demands. Being in business is serious and it is imperative you set your own time expectations yourself.

Once you have your list, give each task two ratings:

1. <u>Ease to complete</u> - 1 being easy to do, 10 being a difficult task
2. <u>Importance to the business</u> - 1 being low priority, 10 being high priority

Then add your ratings together.

For example:

Task - Phoning customers - 1 in terms of difficulty, 10 in terms of high importance = 11

Focus on tasks that most impact the business with the highest priority, which are the ones with the <u>highest</u> totals.

Reacting to every situation as it is presented, is never an efficient way to operate, unless, of course, it is an emergency.

CHAPTER 11

FREQUENCIES

The first few seconds of any encounter are the most important and it's your frequency that people are picking up on. It can be the difference between people coming toward you or staying well away!

I don't want to sound too "woo woo" so you may want to think of your frequency in terms of the way you sparkle (or not) when you enter the room or a conversation.

In sales we need to create a good connection fast. When we are bright eyed and welcoming with a warm smile, people are much more likely to engage in conversation with us.

This was something I personally struggled with because apparently, I have what is commonly called a "resting bitch face" which basically means that when I am not smiling I really look quite grumpy. It happens when I disappear inside myself and most particularly when I am not outwardly engaging in conversation.

To sell better we literally need to 'fizz' in front of people, through our frequency and vibrations.

In fact, my first experience with the subject of frequencies was when I was looking for a solution to my lifelong sleep issues. I had tried all the standard advice and I ended up attending an overnight sleep clinic, plugged into a unit for analysis, with 27 wires glued to various parts of my body.

Three weeks later the results were in and I found out that my Cortisol level was overriding my Serotonin level by some measure which meant my body was in a constant state of fight or flight.... But why?

Armed with this new information, I started digging around for ways to lower my Cortisol and the most effective solution I found was by using Theta brainwave music to change my brain frequency.

> Described very basically, vibration in physics refers to the oscillations, or the back and forth motion of the particles of a body or medium. The number of vibrations per second is known as the frequency and is measured in Hertz (1Hz = 1 vibration/cycle = a complete wave of alternating current per second).
>
> Frequency refers to the number of vibrations/cycles in a unit of time and the rate at which current changes direction per second. Frequencies relate to many things in our world and the universe.
>
> Theta waves resonate at 3.5-7.5 Hertz. They are associated with a deeply relaxed state of mind, dreaming, meditation and prayer. A daydreamer or those slipping between being asleep and awake enters the Theta state which also relates to the subconscious mind.

Thus, I became more and more interested in energies and frequencies and how important it is for us to understand how we are showing up to people in a frequency sense.

GIVING OFF GOOD VIBRATIONS

Everything in the universe is made up of molecules vibrating at different speeds. When we 'pick up good vibrations' what does that actually mean?

Whenever we present ourselves or our business, the rule of sales is that you need to speak in a vibration that attracts your audience to take action. This means projecting our subject matter with confidence and enthusiasm. Your audience has to be really sure that you are the person who holds the solution to their problem. If you look unsure or sound unsure, they won't buy. Certainty is what we are looking for here. Think about when you are the buyer. You want to know the product or service will do the job it is intended for. Your audience has exactly the same requirement from you.

To many this means being over-the-top and shouty to get your message across. It is not about volume; it is about velocity of enthusiasm and certainty that your solution works, and your offer is an exact fit for what they need and is too irresistible to ignore.

When it comes to selling, we need to match the vibration of what we want to manifest. If we want to manifest right fit customers who will take action and strive to thrive, then we must create that same energy of 'can do' mentality, not 'can't do because of x,y,z'. Use your own high intent frequency to create, rather than trying to imitate someone else's words or ways. Use your own knowledge and enthusiasm sprinkled with your own wisdom and magic. Never try to sell anything when feeling low or in low vibration and push the process. It doesn't work.

Whilst considering good vibrations, we also need to consider the delivery platform method you use to present and attract your right fit customers as that will have a direct effect on your personal energy level for sure. Pivotal to delivery of your subject matter, is understanding what platform you are best suited to. If you feel real pressure presenting to the camera, then don't do it!

Explore your options.

If you already do public speaking, is that from a stage to real people with whom you can really resonate and get your message across?

Or perhaps you would feel more comfortable creating slides and providing a voice over, then a Q & A session afterwards.

Maybe you hate the idea of presenting from stage even at a small venue, but feel that Zoom meetings or webinars suit your smaller audience until you begin to scale.

Or perhaps you're considering starting a podcast, in which case consider being someone's guest first. There are lots of ways open to you, but you need to experiment and get a feel for what is the best fit for you rather than be blinkered to one method or indeed by someone else's preference. Again, this demands you listen to your inner voice and where it feels comfortable to speak.

During the 6 Figure Sales Coaching Club sessions, we explore some of these options by practising with small, fun projects to ease the nerves. Then when my students come to the day of presenting their big offer, they know what to expect and have confidence to deliver effectively.

Do not get distracted by others telling you to stretch outside your comfort zone; you are probably doing enough of that already. Find the pieces that work together for you rather than work against your biology. You will do a much better job.

When we are overstretched, negative thoughts creep into our minds, imposter syndrome creeps in and before you know where you are, you are in freeze mode unable to think or speak.

By increasing your own vibration, you resonate with the energy of the universe and thus into an abundance creator whereby opportunities appear, valuable connections with strangers happen synergistically and we experience what we all call 'luck'. By living in higher vibration, you attract more of what you desire in life with ease.

STAY CONNECTED TO YOUR ENERGY

Let's refer back to Albert Einstein again....

"Everything is energy and that's all there is to it. Match the frequency of the reality you want and you cannot help but get that reality. It can be no other way. This is not philosophy. This is physics."

Thinking back again to all the roles we play in life, it is no wonder we are often stuck in our heads with worrying, organising and planning rather than in our hearts and being in flow, being creative and moving in each moment.

We place excessive demands on mind processing to race through our task list. This results in a massive disconnect between heart and mind. It is not us at our best.

This is the very moment when women can sound more masculine and pushy because they are coming from the masculine mind and not the feminine heart.

So, keeping the heart><mind path uninterrupted, is really important so that we remain in balance with our best energy. Of course, there are times when women need to use masculine energy too but best to use it with a feminine overlay which is softer and more collaborative.

ENTHUSIASM IS INFECTIOUS

Why is enthusiasm so important in sales?

It is very difficult to feel good about a purchase if it is not backed by a 24k smile.

All of us enjoy validation for our decisions, especially where money is concerned. Sometimes we are making a cheeky little purchase that we feel a bit guilty about making or we have been courted by the promise of an amazing bargain we found impossible to refuse. Whatever the reason, we all need to feel good about having made that decision to buy. Imagine a salesperson with a laissez-faire attitude, not really bothered about you or the sale. It wouldn't feel good would it?

Conversely, how does it feel when a salesperson joins the process of the sale with you?

Feminine energy loves to join in by sharing the problem, being involved in debating the potential choices and solutions.

Women nurture the sale whereas men tend toward being more prescriptive because the male buyer wants a more prescriptive sell. Women like to discuss and ponder their choices, to reveal all their options that are constituent parts of what women call 'shopping'.

I had an interesting experience this week when I went to buy a new jacket. I entered what I felt was like a lion's den. The sales assistants were literally prowling around, over offering advice. Three different assistants approached me to show me options in the first 3 minutes and after I had already affirmed I would just like to browse for a while and that I would ask for help if needed. This is not service. This is pressure.

Feminine energy hates this type of approach. It felt pushy, manipulative and I certainly didn't feel I was receiving service. They concentrated on getting the sale rather than providing the service.

I left with nothing.

Many of us like to be admired in a dress we've selected to wear and feel confident that the price tag will match the value gained. The way we gauge that is by asking for the opinion of others; a friend, mother, daughter. So, if you are a shop owner or assistant in women's retail, for example, you are definitely a key part of the feminine energy sale. By focussing on the money and not on the service is a huge mistake. Women have antennae for spotting this at a mile.

If you are a business owner with female customers, it is imperative you or your team really care about providing excellent service with a smile. Remember too that as the owner, you set the standard for others to follow, so make sure you enter your workspace with the most buoyant mindset every day, set firmly on your service dial.

Others are watching!

Now it's your turn:

What is the first impression that you give to your customers?

What do they see that perhaps you don't?

What is their experience of what you offer?

Enthusiasm, as we all know, is infectious.

BUILD RELATIONSHIPS

DON'T CHASE TRANSACTIONS

PART 2

THE METHOD

EXPECT THE BEST IN EVERYTHING

CHAPTER 12

OPENING THE FLOW STATE

As we start with The Method, it's important to differentiate between what works and what doesn't when it comes to selling. The best way to help someone is not with advice, it's with questions that open up their minds and lead to you earning the right to introduce new choices to them.

People have come to you to resolve a specific pain or a challenge but before you can do this, you must hear them speak freely, to find that window into their minds. You cannot do this by imposing your own views on them. They are stuck in their current repetitive thoughts and patterns and beliefs. This is not where they'll find the answers to their pains and it's why they're knocking on your door for potential solutions.

You need to expand their choices but you can only do this by coaching them through the thought processes required to get to that starting gate. Meet them where they are right now and coax out the golden nuggets.

My work over the years has drawn me into the many different ways of selling but what I found the most valuable, was how to duplicate the thinking and results of exceptional achievers.

I spend a lot of time speaking to and working with entrepreneurs and if you're a business owner, the impact of this advanced thinking knowledge can have the most profound effect. The great news is that you can apply this to any area of your life but it all starts with your thinking. Your life is driven by your actions and your actions are driven by your thoughts.

We need to fine-tune our thinking to position ourselves to achieve extraordinary results. This is your fast track to being super successful, together with a selling style I call Flow State Selling, enabling our personal and business lives to work synergistically. It's the secret to success in sales.

In Flow State Selling there are two energies we work with. Flow and Firm Up. Each has 3 simple steps that need to be taken in order to generate the result called A SALE :-)

Following my system, we spend the majority of our time in the FLOW state. Why? Because this is where the magic happens. People open up and tell us their troubles, their worries and their key issues... in short... the stuff that sales are made of!

So, in order to start Flow State Selling, firstly we need to free ourselves up from limiting thoughts that map us incorrectly into a particular way of thinking.

When something goes wrong, we immediately come up with a likely cause for the issue. We often assume the cause but the cause we select is created by our mind and is not necessarily the correct one. We try to identify a cause quickly by searching our beliefs to avoid uncertainty and try to work out what to do to keep ourselves or in this case our business safe.

For example, let's say you're on a plane and there was really bad turbulence. Often your mind will jump rapidly to interpret the cause.

You may think that the cause could be due to an engine problem and start panicking about the plane itself but it could turn out to be a weather problem. Just because we jump to interpret the cause doesn't mean we're right.

In this circumstance, we need to change the meaning that we've attached to the situation. Just by recognising that we all make judgements on automatic pilot we become consciously aware of our thinking. When we become aware of our thinking we now know this will directly affect the next action we take and how we will feel as a result.

So instead begin by deciding how you want to feel about a situation. In sales, we obviously want to have the best, most positive outcome for our business. We need to avoid that surge of uncertainty or pressure and to keep focused on that feeling of helping someone to achieve their own goals.

This is a mind shift situation and probably flies in the face of everything anyone has ever told you about successful selling but prescriptive sales techniques just make people feel pressured and out of sync. It's like talking to a robot that doesn't really care about your business. Prospects lose their ability to speak freely, to listen and to exchange views with you on how to solve their pain. This can only result in only one outcome, they clam up and then close you down.

Let's look at footballers as a prime example. They attach a different meaning and feeling to when the other side scores. This is a high pressure situation for them, they earn a stack load of cash and they carry the expectations of thousands of fans but they are trained to use that situation as a trigger to change their energy and to get straight back into the match.

The message here is that successful people learn and act from failure; it really isn't the end of the story. We just need a coping strategy and to reframe or revisit our beliefs in what we are facing.

I call this "Changing The Mix". Changing The Mix is where you notice a feeling and do something to change your state. That sometimes means putting on loud music and throwing myself around the lounge in a dancing frenzy for a couple of minutes (sometimes even with my pseudo microphone hairbrush in hand!), taking myself off for a brisk walk in the fresh air, or even bonging on my amazing Nepalese singing bowl. The important thing is to realise you are feeling fear or anxiety or pressure and to do something to Change The Mix.

Here's an exercise for you:

What 3 actions can you take to Change The Mix when you need to?

What could you do to change your energy and state?

Changing The Mix allows you to open up a clear channel to begin to sell in flow.

If you find it quite awkward to follow a sales process or don't consider yourself as a salesperson, then it's important that you relax into it and see yourself as less of a salesperson and more of someone who is there to serve them.

After all, it's just a conversation. By changing your perspective and putting the focus on their needs, this will be the game changer for you and you'll begin to actually enjoy the process.

CHAPTER 13

THE POWERBASE

The most important part of Flow State Selling is to begin by placing your prospect into a position of power. This means letting them speak freely from what I call their power base or comfort zone. This is the place where they are most empowered to speak. They know all the details, all the relevant data surrounding their subject. This is where their ultimate confidence lies and you need to place them on a pedestal and hear them as the expert. Then get ready to hear that passion and enthusiasm in their voice as they move into their power.

Put them into the position of power, don't grab it for yourself by doing all the talking!

The best way to put them in a position of power is to ask open questions.

Open questions are questions that create an answer that is more than just yes or no. The goal here is to find out as much as you can about the potential customer.

Open questions start with:
WHO
WHAT
WHEN
WHERE
HOW
WHY

Avoid asking questions that they can answer with a simple yes or no as these are called closed questions and you won't learn very much from them.

Here is an example of a closed question:

Q: This is a lovely sporty car and I think it'll really suit you won't it?
A: NO!

As you can see, this is taking your sale nowhere! The answer has closed down this sales opportunity.

Contrast this with an example of a much better OPEN question:

Q: What would be the best type of vehicle to accommodate all the family's needs?

A: Well we have 3 children and we all love camping and cycling together so we need a big bike rack on the roof and a large space to fit in us all and our gear.

Open questions, opening up flow state, make the conversation relaxed whilst revealing information and exchanging ideas for a possible solution is what you are aiming for.

Here are a few examples of open questions:

Q: Who has been your biggest influence in life?
Q: What is the biggest lesson you've learnt in business?
Q: When did you first discover you had xyz skill?
Q: Where did you train?
Q: How did you get into this line of work?
Q: Why do you love it?

Using who, what, when, where, how and why, write down a few questions relevant to your audience, so that you have some ready to use next time you are starting a sales conversation.

And here is an important point if you naturally talk a lot or are used to rambling during a conversation.

The issue with talking too much is that it is you doing the talking. You are not learning more vital information about the prospect and we run the risk of sounding like you're just filling space for the sake of it and actually just wasting the prospect's time.

Listen 80%, talk 20%.

Allow the prospect to get into flow and at all costs avoid cutting across their train of thought.

Remember, everyone loves to be listened to!

CHAPTER 14

SCRAP THE SCRIPT – ESPECIALLY WHEN COLD CALLING

The process of making sales can be quite daunting for people and that's why it's important to follow the right method.

And for anyone starting out in sales, there is a real temptation to find a sales script to follow, especially if there is a need to cold call on the telephone. However, by using a script it can sound rather flat because there is no flavour of you. You are the essential but missing piece in this scenario.

I am sure most of us have been exposed to people cold calling on the telephone and very obviously following a script to the 't'. It sounds fake and that's usually because it is fake. The person is not speaking from their centre and adding quirky comments or bits of information so there is no light or shade, no authenticity.

The net result is that prospects won't trust you, there's a mask and they can perceive it.

This is an excellent time for you to get into your own flow and ask:

What real value does my product, service or program bring to my potential customers?

Reading a script can feel very rehearsed and that is why it sounds so contrived and without spontaneity because there is no golden thread to the centre of you.

In a world where we see images of a perfect life, perfect kids and perfect body image, it is interesting that on social media the biggest numbers of viewers and followers are drawn to images and videos that aren't quite perfect and that translates as being achievable by the masses, not just the few.

Be authentic, tap into you and don't worry if things are slightly less than perfect, people will love you for it. Imperfection makes us relatable and thus trustworthy to our audience.

Here's my three-step process to start your call without a script, especially for a cold call:

1. **Preparation**

Prepare for the call you are about to make. Do your research into the background of the business and/or person you are approaching.

Finding a juicy little nugget to drop into the conversation that follows can be key. It translates to the listener that you have been bothered to do your homework about them, that this contact with them really matters to you leaving the recipient of the call refreshingly surprised.

2. Introduction

Next you need to craft an introduction. It needs to be very succinct and it needs to have a question tagged on the end. This is the most critical part of the cold call.

The attention span of listeners is probably down to about 8 seconds nowadays, mainly influenced by the way we have trained ourselves to browse and scroll online, so you have limited time to make a great first impression. So, what you are looking for is an attention-grabbing question.

For example, in 1990, I was hoping to win a large contract with a multinational organisation to supply nationwide IT contractors. I noticed at the bottom of the tender document was the actual file path where it was stored, which included the word 'Peregrine' so when I cold called the head of procurement I said:

"Hello Dave, it's Suzi Seddon here from xyz company. I didn't know you were a bird watcher!"

This got Dave's attention who was more than a little curious how on earth I had found this out. So, by the time we had exchanged a sentence or two about how, he was already smiling and that phone call led to a £30 million contract. But it all started with that sentence.

3. Open Questions

Once an initial connection has been established with a prospect, move on to asking open questions so that you really understand if you have a great solution for what they seek. This is the positioning piece.

It is not the time to attempt to close. It is the time to nurture the new connection, aiming to move to a relationship where you won't feel like you're making another cold call the next time you make contact.

Start by perceiving the situation from your potential customer's perspective. Put yourself in their position and think about the different products you would be interested in if you were them hearing about the range of products you are selling.

Resist going into aggressive sales mode because as we covered earlier with energy, pushy sales don't work.

When we scrap the script, we are inviting our intuition to tap into that moment in time by listening more than talking but spotting opportunities to garner rapport.

Top Tip:

When using open questions, it can be a good idea to record your telephone sales calls to study and learn from them. You can then spot patterns in what you say, hear the type of consistent questions coming from prospects and allows you to critique yourself. Could you have asked better questions? Did you answer them effectively? Did you achieve the objective of the call?

STAND OUT IN A SEA OF SAMENESS

CHAPTER 15

UNCOVERING THE CORE ISSUES

There is a massive need for simplification and being able to explain to prospects exactly what your product, program or service will do for them.

When we haven't refined our sales approach, we can get way too wordy and this just confuses people.

We need to craft a clear and concise message about what our product is, how it works and/or what it will do for our prospects.

I aim to provide you with a blueprint for exactly how to do this and for you to come away with your own winning formula.

So many people are literally petrified when it comes to selling and get really self-conscious. But we need to understand that the person in front of us really wants to hear what we have to say, so our focus needs to be firmly on them, outward looking and not on ourselves. If we focus on ourselves, this is the territory of self-consciousness and it's not where we need to be.

Selling in flow works through these challenges and entirely repositions your thinking, giving you that explosion of confidence that ripples from you so that you won't even notice that you're actually selling.

We know there are systems and programs out there promoting complicated sales processes that many women regard as sleazy, pushy and manipulative.

Not only is it really difficult to sell something when you're concentrating on using some technique or other but you can lose that elixir of authenticity and enthusiasm that spills from you when you're talking freely and passionately about what you're selling.

If you haven't gathered already from the content of this book, there's absolutely no need for complicated processes and techniques. It's all about relationship building and getting yourself and your prospect into flow.

When selling empowers the client rather than the salesperson, you both win.

Your life is driven by your actions and your actions are driven by your thinking.

Understanding how your brain and everyone else interprets information is fundamental to getting into the Flow State. It's like driving down a highway with traffic easily flowing in both directions and the seamless ability for traffic to join the flow. This is what your selling protocol needs to look like.

The hurdle that many women face after asking open questions is that they jump to conclusions too quickly. We often believe our quick thinking will get us the sale faster but it won't.

We need to learn to listen much more and let our prospect get into Flow State too.

So many of us don't sit in the centre of our being when we talk to prospects. It's like we've had a personality transplant and totally unlike when we are relaxed and comfortable with friends. The minute the word sales pops into our head so does our alter ego. This is the pushy side of the personality and it rears its head when we are unsure of how to approach the sales process. Our language shrinks, our sentences shrink and this translates to our prospects as pressure.

Instead, the goal is to relax, listen and keep asking lots of open questions.

Maybe you're reading this book because you're fed up with losing sales. People seem interested and then they don't buy and you don't know why.

Does this resonate with you?

The usual reason is because you haven't uncovered the potential customers' Shopping List.

The Shopping List is their list of needs and wants. This is a critical part of selling.

If you don't do a thorough job of this, you'll make life a whole lot more difficult for yourself when it comes to offering your final diagnosis of their problem and your solution.

Remember also to listen to the order in which your prospect discusses what is on their shopping list because typically the most important item is the one that they mention first or most often.

By asking lots of questions you are cutting through all the noise, directing the flow of the conversation and getting to the nitty gritty of what the prospect is struggling with. Additionally, you are positioning yourself on their team, searching for the solution with them. If they consider you as being on their team, then logically you are less likely to be considered as a salesperson.

They may want to buy a car and you could find out:

- Do they want a sunroof?
- Do they want it for City driving or motorway driving?
- Have they got half a dozen kids or none?
- Do they need a roof rack?
- Do they need to cater for their doggy?
- Do they need to cater for an elderly relative?
- Are they keen to limit their footprint?
- Is anyone else going to drive the car? e.g. son/daughter?
- Is reliability at the top of their list of needs?

Remember these are not the questions you'll be asking them. You'll want to ask them open questions that help you find out this information about what they need or want. Think about some really good questions that could shine a light on what you sell. By seeding your prospect's mind, they will likely revisit these when reviewing if your solution is for them.

If you haven't uncovered this information and more then you have very little chance of closing the deal with them. This is because you may be basing your actions upon your own assumptions and not hard information. Sometimes we conclude that a lost sale is because of one thing, when it is actually due to another.

Instead we want to have the best chance of closing the sale by doing the best we can on uncovering their shopping list.

SLOW DOWN TO SPEED UP

The reason why people often reject the advances of a salesperson is because they feel pushed and uncomfortable. They feel backed into a corner or even worse, backed into that corner far too quickly. This throws the customer into that uncertainty we spoke about earlier. They have accessed their own belief system and concluded in double quick time that unless they get out of this situation very quickly, they'll have purchased something they don't really want or need. So, they panic and run or worse still, when people are really pushed, they feel obligated to buy. This can result in resentment, bad press, as they tell all their friends how awful the experience was, and invariably a refund or cancellation. All in all, a big waste of time and energy for both parties.

Whenever we think of selling, we naturally think of closing the deal but what we really need to concentrate on is closing the deal elegantly. It's important that our prospective buyer doesn't feel any pressure to buy whatsoever. The job of a salesperson is to establish what is on the prospect's shopping list by asking lots of questions to unlock more expansive thinking that feels easy to share, to diagnose if there is a good fit with what you offer and only then to encourage the prospect toward the sale step-by-step, so the decision process feels natural and balanced.

You can't rush through this part of the sales conversation.

Uncovering the core issue is vital if you are to get to the point of making a sale.

We want our potential customers to feel empowered and safe so they can open up about what will motivate them to move forward or what is holding them back.

MAP YOUR OFFER TO THEIR ISSUES

By now you will have a really clear idea about what your potential customer thinks they want but also what they need.

You will know when they want it or when they need it.

You know what budget constraints they have and importantly if they are the decision maker for their business and if not, you will have uncovered other parties involved in making the decision.

You have uncovered any hidden agenda they may have or information that was missing earlier in your discussions.

You have placed them in a position of power to advise you what is happening in their business and what issues they face.

You have placed yourself in the position of the person 'learning' and 'listening' and 'questioning'.

So, start to look at the situation from your prospect's perspective and think about which of your products, programmes and services could be a great option for them.

But resist the urge to adapt what you offer to different price points on an individual basis. It is a recipe for trouble and will only succeed in you getting confused during the pitch of your offer, or a raft of dissatisfied customers who feel duped demanding refunds.

What you can do is offer clearly different products, programmes or services aimed at different points in your ideal customer journey. Or you could offer an introductory offer that solves one pain point they face, or a one-day workshop or even a Challenge that focuses on one element in the journey.

Concentrate on offers that encapsulate what your ideal customer needs as they move through the different stages of their business and leave them to opt in or not for what you offer.

SIMPLIFY TO AMPLIFY

CHAPTER 16

THE PITCH

The pitch is where you present your opportunity to your potential customer and it can only be done when you really understand their challenges, needs and wants.

It is not about blabbing out of control or filling space because it sounds like more value. That will only result in a woolley and unstructured message.

Your pitch needs to be tight, clear and concise. So, let's look at what needs to be in it.

There are multiple in-depth steps to designing a finely tuned sales pitch because it needs to be on point, clear and concise and you need to really dig deep into the questions your prospective customer needs answering. Start thinking about…

Do they **need** what you sell?

What is it actually? e.g. a system/process etc

How does it work?

Why will it work for them?

Let's deal with some high-level questions to get your thoughts flowing:

What is your product?
What is it about?
Why does it work?
In what markets does it work?
What results can they expect?
What's my background or experience?
How will I back up my claims?
What are my audience's biggest pain points?

PRESENTING OPTIONS

So, you have sorted out what value you bring to customers; the uniqueness of your business, proof and reassurance with the facts and figures, graphs, awards and existing clients to back things up.

Let's talk about your secret sauce; YOUR expert knowledge.

You know your business better than anyone. You've grown with it, experiencing all of its growing pains and successes. There is no one better positioned than you to sell it.

Remember being in flow, isn't about delivering an elevator pitch. Far from it! They are great for networking events but that's all.

Real people want to meet real people, not a hard-nosed salesperson just spurting one-way spiel telling you what to think. Sales today is a collaborative process, it's about authenticity and working out the best solution you can offer and backing it up with the proof, facts and most of all results.

Formal in front of a whiteboard, or informal over coffee, whichever way you choose to go through the options, there will be no facts more important than the results you can bring someone, the transformation and the solution to their problems. This is what they'll have a real hunger for.

If you can show results you've achieved for a similar business then that will be a huge magnet to your solution. You're beginning to layer proof. Proof that you have a solution, proof that the solution fits the criteria you've discussed and identified.

Softly, softly is the language of selling in flow.

Let's take a look at a couple of examples of the way you could open things up:

"So, I'm looking at ways I can help you move forward. One of my products helps you reach a mass audience in one session (give details). When are you hoping to start promoting your product?"

OR

"One of my products focuses on growing your email list and teaches you how to nurture your prospects – how does that sound?"

You are now mapping your product options to your potential customer's Shopping List of needs and wants. Most importantly, you are getting a feel for how receptive they are to your suggestions. This is when you bring back in those little value statements to underpin your solution.

Think about how this potential customer can grow with you. Does one of your products lead naturally to another that could really help them towards achieving their goals over time with you?

The best customer you can have is a repeat customer!

DIAGNOSIS AND THE WAY FORWARD

When a prospect is considering your product, service or program, their unconscious mind knows what they are currently using or doing and that it brings significant benefit to them.

They won't give that benefit up until you replace it with something that gives an equal or greater benefit.

So, having uncovered the issues and identified what is on your prospects Shopping List, which is made up of what they believe they need and want, you can finally present your solutions based on what you have discovered.

You can do this by replaying their story as it's been revealed to you and then offer 2 to 3 features or benefits that fit each pain point on their list as a more effective solution.

A feature is an essential function of a product or service.

A benefit refers to how that feature may benefit the buyer.

This may be in terms of efficiency, faster results or a myriad of other better solutions for what they seek but all will be directly attributed to a specific pain point and will address that issue.

Presenting your solutions with an air of enthusiasm and energy is critical because this wide-eyed excitement for your product, program or service is what will inspire your potential customer as a real choice for them.

Think about when you've been to a restaurant and the waiter took time to run through the complete menu with you, really explaining and describing things rather than just plonking it down in front of you and walking away. If you can demonstrate your product and engage all of your prospect's senses, it's the easiest way ever to 'close a sale'.

So, if you have done the work and exercises I've outlined, you'll be in a great position to present your solution and ask for the sale.

Don't forget that some people are very driven by data and need to see all the figures and if you like 'proof'. It is just the way they are wired. I recommend having some of this data to hand when you're in a sales conversation so you can access it easily.

So, it is important to provide your solution as a written proposal too.

A written proposal is a brief document that summarises your product/program or service. It includes bulleted information on:

- Name of Product/Program/Service
- Length of the Program if applicable
- Price Options including PayPlan Options
- A short descriptor of what it is and who it's for.
- What is included such as an On-Boarding call, 1:1 Coaching Calls, Access to a Template Vault, Access to Support.

A written proposal can be used to follow up a cold call or face to face meeting. This then generates another opportunity to follow up the sending of the written proposal a few days later.

When creating a written proposal, I recommend producing it in pdf format so that you can send quickly to your prospects with a voice note on WhatsApp but you can also include it on your website if appropriate.

Ensure you have created it ready to send via email or a link via WhatsApp as soon as you have discussed it with your prospect. Never assume just telling someone is enough!

So, to help you, I have added a simple diagram of The Method; being my Flow State Selling System. Print it, copy it, and put it up somewhere you pass regularly, so that it really engrains into your mind, the steps you need to take. This is your blueprint to follow and you will always know the next step you need to take.

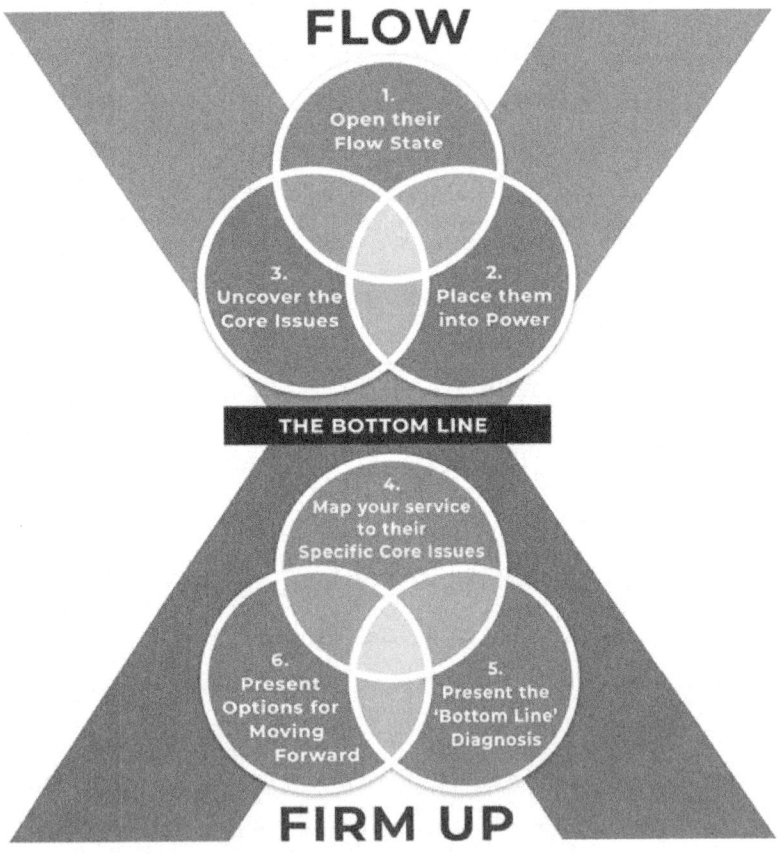

*A coloured printable version is available at
https://suziseddon.com/resources/

CHAPTER 17

PACKAGING YOUR VALUE

When we talk about presenting our solution, we need to think about our value.

We gain experience on an on-going basis. Every day you're becoming better and better at what you do but we forget how much we have to offer and this results in us not putting a true value against our expertise.

If ever you're not sure or you need a boost, ask other people who know you and your work, what they think you are really great at? You'll be surprised what people notice. Building self-worth is key to charging what you're worth.

Charging what we are worth is about understanding our true value.

Another way to look at the value you offer is to consider the impact on the prospect of not resolving their issue. What would solving the problem be worth to them? It could have a huge financial impact on them, thus placing your value as an essential investment.

As humans we move away from pain, more than we do toward pleasure.

By focusing on price, you will attract price conscious potential customers. Focus on value not on price and communicate your value to prospects.

Demonstrate and discuss all the value you bring and when you confidently outline your pricing, this will make all the difference.

ENCOURAGE ACTION TAKERS

No one wants to put out a product or service that isn't used. After all, what is the use of 'shelf help?' as one of my friends put it. So, rewarding those who take action is a no brainer. This could simply be an impromptu surprise and delight telephone call or an offer to review something for them. Without action, inaction rules and that won't take your customers toward their goal.

So, we need to add some 'nice to have' but not essential bonuses with our offer. Audiences love the idea of something for nothing! The first secret with bonuses is to make sure you add something that is really useful to the central offer you are making, but is not an essential part of it. It serves to sweeten the deal thus making your offer irresistible.

Another secret is to tie the bonus to prospects taking fast action to buy, for example making it available for a very limited period or limit to the first 6 people to take up the offer.

When making an offer there are 3 ways to help focus the prospects mind. You can limit the offer by:

TIME (e.g. offer expires at midnight)

Time restriction for your offer avoids running the risk of inertia or lack of action by your potential customers. Some of them just need a time box to really focus on the value you are offering but only for a limited period.

PAYMENT OPTIONS (e.g. 1 pay, 3 pay or 12 pay options)

Payment options can encourage new buyers that wouldn't normally be able to sign up due to cost. So, by offering a range of options, you are more likely to appeal to these buyers.

Pay in Full (sometimes referred to as 1Pay) provides the customer with your best offer, because all of the payment is up front. Alternatively, you can offer 3Pay (pay once a month for 3 months or bi-monthly for a 6-month course for example). You can even offer a 12Pay option whereby the customer pays monthly at the beginning of each month. Which option you use will really depend on how much the overall product/program or service is. Be aware that with 12Pay that this is the most likely option to renege on the contract between you, so beware of offering all your content front loaded toward the beginning of the 12 months.

ATTENDEES (e.g. only 6 spaces)

A scarcity limit operates in a similar way to payment options. However, this set of buyers is not motivated necessarily by cost, they just want to take up your offer, especially if you have offered a Fast Action Bonus for the first 6 people. So, this is where cost isn't the deciding factor. Action is.

Overall, including limits for urgency and scarcity can be a great way to encourage action takers. Which one you use is down to you but I caution you to stick to either Payment Plans or Scarcity - don't mix both because it becomes complicated for the prospective customer to decide, especially if you have a timer ticking down to the offer disappearing at the end of the presentation/workshop.

Make it easy for them to take action, don't complicate it.

And finally, probably most importantly, don't lose sight of an offer that converts. It's very tempting to swiftly move on to the next thing. Don't change it. Just rinse and repeat. At some point the sales for it will probably dwindle but that can be two years down the track. You cannot keep offering exclusive discounts and bonuses for a limited time and then keep them open for longer, that's not honest or authentic. But when there is an offer that is working, keep it available. Don't try to fix what isn't broken.

DON'T LOSE SIGHT OF WHAT WORKS

CHAPTER 18

BUILDING TRUST

Building trust is a very personal thing. Some people want lots of testimonials and case studies. Others want data and statistics.

Both essentially lead to them trusting that you have the solution for what they need.

Earlier in the book we talked about opening up Flow State and building rapport and trust right from your first contact with a prospect. Remember that if you have built that initial connection and you have done a great job of asking questions, you will arrive at a place where the prospect has no more questions. Think about how you can help your prospect gain trust. Could you offer to put them directly in touch with a couple of customers? This puts them in control. They can ask what it's like to work with you. They can even ask how effective your product or service is.

Let's build out a bit more detail that you may be asked for.

Why should potential customers trust you, your solution and what you are offering?

How many years have you been in business?

What awards have you won?

Are you the specialists in your marketplace?

How quickly can they get results from you?

What case studies and testimonials can you show them?

BODY LANGUAGE

Body language is also important when you're selling. The fastest way to change your own state of mind is to change your physiology. I believe it was an American President who used this tactic when 'stalemate' had locked negotiations. The stuck energy was soon broken with a walk outside around the park in the fresh air before returning to the negotiating table with a fresh perspective and back into a state of flow. So, changing your physiology can be a really effective tool to use when selling.

Changing state does not only apply to how you are personally feeling, it can also apply to changing the state of a negotiation you are engaging in, especially if things feel a little stuck or progression is slow.

For example, think about the last time you went to buy a car. Showrooms tend toward feeling clinical with their shiny floors and shiny cars and wide open spaces. It really can feel quite exposing as a prospective customer. Most women don't enjoy this type of environment, favouring a more nurtured approach where they can ask the salesperson questions with confidence. This feeling of looming pressure is often down to the body language of the sales person. Typically, and traditionally the car showroom has been an ostensibly male domain. Women don't generally enjoy the prescriptive sales process, where the salesman rushes over to you, business card in hand, ready to explain or tell you all about it. Whatever "it" is because usually they haven't done their exploratory questions to really understand your needs and wants; your shopping list. It all feels way too pushy, especially if they are trying to get you to sign up there and then. Their body language is screaming 'just sign the contract' moving in to close you as soon as possible.

Conversely, imagine that you are considering buying a fast car. Wouldn't it be great to be invited to meet the salesperson at a racetrack; to see the speed, to hear the roar of the engine, to ride inside the car and feel the excitement! Space and freedom without feeling so pressured to buy is essential. It's a world away from how many garages sell cars today; yes, they may have one or maybe two of the elements covered but when you can give a potential customer a total sensory experience, this is when the magic happens and the sale takes care of itself.

Similarly, and particularly when you're on video or livestream, you can communicate an awful lot with hand gestures, like tapping your head when you're talking to your audience about top of head ideas or placing your hand on your heart when you ask them the question "how does it feel?"

When you ask your audience to take an action, like switching off their mobile phone, you can show your own phone and switch it off in front of them whilst requesting them to follow suit. This trains your audience to follow your lead and importantly when it comes to asking them to click the buy button, they're more likely to do it.

Consider for a moment how you can switch things up in your own business and inject new positive energy into your sales process.

Body language is a massive subject in and of itself but essentially in sales we are talking about ensuring our physiology doesn't either offend or feel oppressive.

It's about open, accepting postures that don't shut people down. For example, if you are displaying your wares in public, don't stand behind the table, stand to the side. Arms or legs crossed is a very closed posture that signals you don't want to interact, so a disaster if you are trying to sell.

Don't trap people in your shop by making it difficult for them to browse without pressure and if you are running a stand at an Exhibition, allow flow in and around the stand at all times. I once saw a perfect example of this at a gift fair. There was a stand selling mechanical toys of all sorts and they had a train on a track that ran around the top of the stand. It was like a magnet to all the kids (and the big kids too) but most of all, the train served to bring people toward the stand because of the flow it offered around it and people felt inspired to start chatting because the focus wasn't on them!

CHAPTER 19

EMBRACE REJECTION & BUILD RESILIENCE

If you expect to get things right from the start, you are probably going to have a surprise. You may be the luckiest person alive if you get it right from the get go and get all the moving pieces together but at some point, you'll face some level of rejection in sales.

Rejection is a part of selling. It's par for the course.

No one enjoys rejection but the way to handle it is to embrace it and reframe it in your head. If you consider that it would be a tall order to get things right from the start, then please also consider that any rejection serves to get you to dial in harder to what your right fit customer is searching for. As you start to count things out, you can begin to see what they really need from you and what your irresistible offer needs to deliver.

Building resilience to rejection is imperative. As women we are more likely to take rejection personally but it's important to remain objective about this. If you begin to take things personally, this is when you will begin to over analyse what went wrong.

Just know you won't win everything you pitch for. You may learn the rejection reason but often there will be an external reason that affects the decision at the last minute, so you may never learn the reason why. Accept it and move on.

The faster you move on to your next prospect, the less attention you will pay to soul searching the reason why you lost this one.

This is why in the 6 Figure Sales Coaching Club, we come together online once a week to share and resolve challenges met in the previous week. It is all very well to go on a course for a number of days and often leave elated and excited, with hope for the future but then home alone again, questions and doubts begin to creep in to sabotage our efforts.

To mitigate this, I became a strong believer in supporting my students via a private community because it's so hard to absorb all of the stuff we've learnt in a short period of time and apply it without forgetting pieces in the framework that could be the hinge to move the door for you.

There are also times that students share their rejections too. Everyone in the community contributes thoughts, ideas and encouragement to keep moving forward. The faster you move through bad news the better. The more you keep turning it over in your mind, the more stuck you will remain.

The power of sitting amongst people who understand what you're going through is invaluable, especially at a time when so many women are solopreneurs and without the input of anyone else who is invested in their business as they are. In many ways it also helps you build resilience because you are immersed with people who are actively building a business just like you. They have faced or are facing the same challenges, so sit amongst them and learn and support each other. Learn from your own mistakes, take yourself out of the situation, counsel the opinion of others and return once you have a way forward in mind.

When it comes to pitching your offer the best advice I can give you is to practice, practice, practice. This is one of THE major mistakes I see.

Too many salespeople like to rely on 'winging it'. Make sure you know your offer, your payment plan options, your bonuses and all the relevant details a prospect could ask you. You just dilute your efforts if you can't answer these questions right at the very point of decision.

We women are sensitive souls and when we receive criticism or rejection we feel it in our hearts. The more you practice, invariably the more mind muscle and resilience you build because you are coming from a place of certainty and strength, negating the tendency to waffle or come up with a solution on the spur of the moment.

CHAPTER 20

OVERCOMING OBJECTIONS

Objections are a natural part of the sales process. An objection is really just a test. A test that you know your offer, a test that you have been asking your prospect questions and listening to the answers.

Objections are not rejections, they are just simply not understanding everything yet and they need more clarity. This should also highlight to you that you need, in future, to ask better open questions. Not handling objections well puts up a red flag in the mind of the buyer who is suddenly not sure or not convinced you have the answer to their challenges.

When objections are handled eloquently your prospect feels served. They will feed off your enthusiasm and confidence for what you sell and they will trust you can get them to where they want to be.

The best way to answer any objections or questions raised is:

CONFIDENTLY

The energy of your confidence in your product, program or service and what it can do for the buyer cannot be underestimated. It's hugely important to a buyer who feeds off that confidence. But a word of caution, this needs to be done without a tone of arrogance or cockiness which will have the opposite effect.

FACTUALLY

Have all the facts to hand. They give supporting evidence that your solution works. These could be case studies or articles written, relevant to the marketplace of the buyer.

BRIEFLY

Avoid waffling at all costs. When handling an objection, it translates either to persuasion, which as we know, feels like pressure to buy or that you don't know all the details. Get clear on your facts and stick to them.

TACTFULLY

Sometimes one really does need to be tactful. For example, if you know your prospect is currently dealing with a disreputable supplier, there is no need to tell them this. The very reason they have come to you is that they already know! Acknowledge the issue they are having, then continue to move through the Method I've outlined.

Objections typically happen where there are gaps between your prospect's shopping list and your offer so these gaps need to be filled.

If you are getting a lot of negatives, objections or indecision, then back-up and return to asking more open questions but above all acknowledge and empathise with any objections raised. This is not a time to go through a prescriptive list. Feel your way through what is coming up for the prospect. Help them.

For example, if someone is having an issue with their spouse not supporting their new business, you may offer to speak to the spouse so that they can raise the concerns they have directly. Keep in flow at all times.

Let's start with a selection of objections to uncover some of the more common ones you could be faced with.

Objection 1: "Can I speak to some of your previous clients? I've been burned before."

This is screaming a lack of trust. This could be a lack of trust in similar businesses or more generally about the industry. The first step would be to ask more about what happened, empathise and give reassurance about your own working practices and also by providing testimonials.

Objection 2: "I need to think about it"

This is a classic case of not revealing hidden information that is relevant to the sale. In other words, the prospect in all probability has unanswered questions. Revisit the questions you are asking and expand them relevant to who you are talking to. Prepare for every call by knowing the reason you are calling or meeting and the outcome you want. Link a question to that outcome.

Objection 3: "I can't commit right now" or "I need to check with my partner"

Very often the decision maker remains behind the scenes. Typically, they can be a spouse or a business partner. When you begin asking open questions at the beginning of negotiations, ensure you are talking to the decision maker. Perhaps by asking "who else needs to be involved before a decision can be made?". This is a critical step. Invest time in the person who holds the most influence in the decision to buy. The question to ask yourself is why this person is in front of you and not the decision maker? How do they fit into the organisation? Move away from thinking about how to "lock someone down" and toward allowing flow toward a sale. Take your foot off the gas and concentrate on understanding the challenge and creating rapport between you.

OBJECTIONS OFFER CHANCES FOR CLARITY

CHAPTER 21

SELL, TRACK, CELEBRATE & REPEAT

As soon as you're on a roll with your sales conversations, it's important to start tracking your progress.

Tracking is the only real way you can get a clear helicopter view of what's going on. The great news is that you can get started by using a simple spreadsheet to track a number of metrics.

For example:

The number of leads.

The most productive source of leads.

Lastly, track the number of conversions.

Start there. Then expand the range of metrics you are tracking as your business begins to expand and you test new methods.

If you don't track your data, you run the risk of losing focus on what works and what doesn't over the long run. So, you could be spending money where the data doesn't support doing so.

By tracking your sales activity, you can then use it for comparing your progress against your monthly, quarterly and yearly goals. Test and track, then tweak. The data never lies.

Follow Up

Most business owners don't do enough follow up. They think it feels uncomfortable and too salesy but in fact it's where most sales are made.

Over half of my sales complete during follow up sales conversations.

The fortune really is in the follow up so we need to have a process for following up.

This could be by sending a personalised video on WhatsApp or other social media platforms. Don't be afraid to follow up a number of times.

Interestingly, is it easier today to get attention through sending a surprise and delight gift in the mail than it is a response via email. Consider mailing a Video Card with a recorded message from you on it and a Post It note saying 'press play now'.

The main rule is to always have a reason for making the call. It could be to check they have received your written proposal or that they received their invitation to maybe an event you are running. Maybe you suspect you didn't really get to the bottom of what the prospect was searching for, call and apologise for not doing a good enough job to understand the situation better and ask if you can run through a few additional questions with them. This is much better than re-approaching with no particular reason in mind other than to close the sale.

Celebration

As we've covered already, selling isn't always easy and can take a lot of time, energy and focus. That's why it's so important to celebrate your wins.

Every goal, every micro milestone, reward yourself. The journey of an entrepreneur can be a lonely one so take pride in your achievements and celebrate. Set the reward in line with the monetary value of the sale achieved so the bigger the win, the bigger the reward.

When you've set your goals each month, each quarter and have an overall yearly goal and you start achieving them then go wild and let your hair down!

CHAPTER 22

TRIP WIRES!

We're in the final chapter which means by now we've covered a lot with the sales process.

But what we haven't covered yet are the "what if" scenarios. These are specific examples of what could happen during a sales conversation that normally you wouldn't be prepared for. There are a number of things that can wrong foot you during the sales process but there are a few techniques that may help rescue the sale.

YOU ARE LOSING CONTROL OF THE SALE

You may have progressed right through the process to the point of making the prospect an offer and they are right at the decision point as to whether to go ahead and then one of two things happens:

(a) You sense they are about to close you down; or
(b) They do, in fact, close you down.

In both circumstances it is important to remember:

The prospect needs to be able to save face if they are going to change their mind.

So, you need to bring them back to the point immediately before the decision was made, add some new information thereby enabling them to reconsider their decision.

To do this, you could say:

"Before you make your decision, I'd like for you to consider…" and then add an additional fact or revisit the point of contention.

And it's also important to reflect and consider why it happened.

This situation usually arises from not having done a thorough job of the initial exploratory questions. I would encourage you to refer back to Chapter 13 to practice these open questions again.

Another reason could be that the part of the sales conversation when you are beginning to open up the dialogue, establishing rapport, trust and uncovering all the possible objections up front was possibly rushed. So, do recap Chapter 13 to practice this again.

UNCOVERING A HIDDEN AGENDA

In the world of sales, we sometimes have to be a detective, particularly if you suspect the prospect has a hidden agenda. But how do you know if they do?

This can be quite difficult to spot but essentially watch out for the questions the prospect asks you <u>in context</u> with what you are discussing. For example, a simple question about colour options could reveal that the prospect is only interested if the item comes in a specific colour. So, don't just answer a question on face value, also ask another supplementary question to clarify things better.

The biggest telltale sign is if they keep revisiting a certain topic and cycling through different tactics but with the same end in mind. They likely display a single mindedness and keep approaching the subject from a different angle as if something is being kept from them.

Other signs include awkward body language or eye contact. Of course our female superpowers are superb at spotting this type of behaviour so rely on your gut feeling.

Faced with uncovering their hidden agenda, you can use Check Questions.

Check Questions are questions that help you explore whether you are in the right vicinity or on the right track and that you understand the issue thereby avoiding jumping too quickly to the wrong conclusion or the wrong solution.

For example, imagine walking into a completely dark room and trying to find your way around. You would naturally proceed with caution, carefully trying not to upset any of the furniture. At the same time, you would be feeling your way around the room trying to get your bearings. Once you feel the edge of the table, you know exactly where you are. This is what you are trying to do with a Check Question.

For example:

"So, what you are saying is that you need to build your email list by 10k really quickly so that you can increase your sales faster. Is that correct?"

OR

If I understand you correctly the most important thing to you is X… Is that right?

A second check question is recommended to uncover any further hidden but relevant factors that need to be revealed, for example:

What else could really help you with Y?

These Check Questions can help you to check that your potential customer is still interested and whether it's worth continuing the conversation.

THE BOUNCE QUESTION

Sometimes people close you down during a sales conversation and you have to find a way to keep the dialogue in flow and that can often trip you up. That's the purpose of the Bounce Question.

Prospects don't always give you as much information as you're looking for or they like to play their cards close to their chest and yes, it's their prerogative but it does make your job of understanding their needs and matching them with your products, programmes or services trickier.

So you could ask, for example:

"What's the best thing about working in your line of business?" (follow up as soon as they've answered with…)

"….and what's the worst?"

or

"How does your current accounting system cope with a heavily component based business?"

"… would it be easier if I showed you how our software handles this headache effortlessly?"

This bounces them to think very quickly – firstly about something that troubles them, and then to a solution that completely eliminates the problem. You're taking them from one extreme to the other in seconds and by doing this they are very likely to fall into Flow State very easily.

Here are some more examples to consider:

"Who are the easiest people for you to sell your products/services to?"

"…and who are the most difficult?"

OR

"Where would you like your business to be this time next year?"

"….what will it take to get you there?"

You can learn an awful lot with a bounce question because it takes people off guard. Just remember to keep your language relaxed and friendly – because nobody wants to feel like they are on a Quiz show!

And Lastly My Secret Weapon… AGREE, THEN DISAGREE!

Sometimes it's the case that an important key piece of information has slipped through the net and not been picked up for consideration. Maybe you feel all is lost but I can tell you honestly, this is a retrievable situation using my secret weapon.

Use this if the prospect declares that they don't think your solution is for them, based on what they've heard.

Acknowledge what they have had to say and then serve in the missing information or another benefit to consider.

For example:

'I understand you have reservations about changing your accounting systems and all the upheaval it'll cause…. but before you finally decide, it's worth considering……xyz'

This rewinds their mind back to BEFORE they made the decision to close you down. It pushes the door open again without them having to lose face. Then you can re-address the objection elegantly without losing face either.

…WIN-WIN always wins the day

Hopefully if you've followed the process taught in this book you won't have to use this secret weapon too often but it's good to have in your back pocket if you need it.

CONCLUSION

So, in summary, as a confidence-building exercise, let's reflect on what you now know:

- You have delved deeply into ascertaining your absolute expertise and not just among a list of competencies you have in life.
- You have dialled into your own brand of personal magic; your secret sauce that is unique to you.
- You are clear about who you serve, who you **want** to serve and whether they can afford your product, program or service.
- You are also clear on your values and beliefs that drive the soul of your business and that also dictate who is a great hire for the team and most importantly who is not.
- You have examined and dealt with any mindset blocks you have, including but not limited to, money

beliefs, self-esteem, confidence issues and imposter syndrome.

- You now understand more about your personal energy system and how pivotal it is in selling.
- You have found or started to look for a like-minded community of soul sisters to support your entrepreneurial journey.
- You have started generating targeted content that attracts <u>exactly</u> the people you want to work with.
- You have developed a few good stories to have in your back pocket to emphasize points you are making to prospects.
- Turning to your prospects, you have ascertained who is the decision maker for the business or anyone else who is involved in it.
- You have invited your prospect to speak openly, and you have listened hard to them speaking as the expert and the issues they are facing. By asking lots of open questions, you aim to genuinely understand things from their perspective.
- You have a clear idea of what your prospect thinks they want and, importantly, <u>what they need</u> as their next step. You have reflected on whether you have a great solution for them.
- You have also considered whether they are a great fit as an ideal customer going forward (this is the area of repeat business).

- You now have an easy framework to follow to take your prospects from browsers to buyers without old style pushy sales tactics.
- You really know the mechanics of the offers you are about to make BEFORE you propose them. Clarity over confusion rules the day!
- You know that coming from your centre and being in flow at all times relaxes all parties and enables an easy two-way flow of information that leaves everyone with a good experience.
- You also know that you won't win everything, but you are committed to learning from each experience. You are willing to adapt or change the questions you ask and tweak the offers you make to attract your absolute right-fit customer.
- Lastly, you know how important it is to celebrate your wins and avoid overwhelm with regular self-care and 'me' time to keep yourself internally in flow.

You are developing a sales muscle and it takes time. If you do something every day to practice your skills and move your business forward, you'll be surprised how soon things will begin to change. If you haven't yet done the tasks in https://suziseddon.com/resources/ then now is a great time to start. Like any skill, you need to take on board new knowledge, build out content based on what you have learned, then apply and test, tweak, refine and test again. Where you are with your business today will evolve and probably out of all recognition. Developing a business and thereafter scaling it is an ongoing process but as you develop your sales muscle, it will become stronger, more refined and so will your business.

You are likely to fall into old bad habits along the way and when you do, just know it's because that was your comfort zone, where you used to operate from until we developed your new sales muscle. As I said in Chapter 16, no one ever gives up what they are currently doing until it is replaced by something that gives a greater benefit… you are no different to your customers. The difference here is that this book is in your hands because what you are currently doing isn't working. Maybe you know you're not doing very much but you don't know where to start, or maybe you're still using a few die hard, pushy sales tactics which, by the way, will never work in today's more connected world where savvy buyers appreciate good sales people and won't engage with those who attempt to open negotiations by trying to close. You just need to trust my tried and tested framework and practice, practice, practice.

The one thought I want to leave you with is this… the key to selling in feminine energy is to get into flow, keep selling in flow and enjoy the journey!

SERVE HARD, SELL EASY

INVITATION

Download the freebie guide on 5 Effective Ways to Overcome Imposter Syndrome in Business:
https://suziseddon.com/overcoming-imposter-syndrome/

Join the email list for more tips, inspiration and motivation on:
https://suziseddon.com/subscribe/

Attend the weekly group Club sessions run by me on Zoom, to mastermind your questions with our Club community. Join The 6 Figure Sales Coaching Club here: https://suziseddon.com/coaching-club/

If you want to continue our journey together, join the Sell Like A Woman 12-month Immersion Program here: https://suziseddon.com/work-with-suzi

Printed in Great Britain
by Amazon